The Mushroom Farm
and other reflections from a spiritual journey

Written by Reverend John R. Dolan

Illustrations by Paul J. Egel

The Mushroom Farm- 2nd Edition, 2011

Copyright © John R. Dolan 2009, 2011

Signalman Publishing 2011
www.signalmanpublishing.com
ISBN: 978-1-935991-26-7 (paperback)

Unless otherwise noted, Scripture quotations are from the New Revised Standard Version Bible, copyright © 1989 by the division of Education of the National Council of Churches of Christ in the U.S.A., and are used by permission.

Scripture quotations and other excerpts included as Appendix 1 are taken from the Book of Common Prayer, 1979 and the Revised Common Lectionary, Episcopal Church U.S.A.

Some proper names of persons living at the time of writing have been changed for reasons of privacy. Other names of living persons have been used with their express permission.

All rights reserved. No part of this publication may be reproduced, stored in a retrieval system, or transmitted, in any form or by any means without the prior written permission of the author, nor be otherwise circulated in any form of binding or cover other than that in which it is published and without a similar condition being imposed on the subsequent purchaser.

www.webstarts.com/johndolan

"Book is delightful"
-Rt. Rev. Jeffrey Lee, Diocesan Bishop of Chicago

"Real and meaningful"
-Ven Elaine Bellis, Archdeacon of Chicago

"Dolan's acute ability to perceive the Divine revealed in the encounters and seeming chance events that overtake us day by day, is a much needed reminder that life is a constant process of revelation, if only we have eyes to see and ears to hear. This collection of personal reflections bears eloquent witness to the fact that the One who meets us in the pages of scripture, can do so as well during rush hour on the London Underground."

-Most, Rev. Frank Tracy Griswold, Former Presiding Bishop, Episcopal Church USA

"A book for a quiet read when one wishes to reflect unto oneself."

-Mr. Nigel Calder, Llandaff, Wales

CONTENTS

Page

7-9	Foreward
11-14	In the midst of the storm, God is with us
15-18	Gifts for those in need reveal His glory
19-25	Turning over the stress of living to Jesus Christ
26-31	The relationship between faith and God's mercy
32-37	We are all equal in God's eyes
38-42	Worship Christ, the King of heaven and earth
43-47	You also should do as I have done to you
48-50	God's love transcends all human conditions
51-56	Growth through love and obedience
57-60	The power arising from humility
61-64	On even the darkest day, hope abounds
65-68	Being caught in traps of our own making
69-73	Be alert! Evil may be lurking behind any door
74-77	God provides a full measure for all of us; no favoritism
78-83	A sense of urgency to invest our talents to do God's work
84-89	Risking your personal safety for your faith in Jesus Christ
90-94	Wait and trust in the Lord
95-99	Any pursuit in life calls for moderation except one's love of Jesus Christ

100-104	Stereotyping hides the loving nature of God
105-108	No free lunches in this life
109-114	God's gifts are for the benefit of all God's creatures
115-118	Be alert to challenges to our Christian values
119-123	Spiritual growth nurtured in faith from the spiritual seed
124-128	Be generous with God's unique gifts given to us
129-134	The power and glory of compassion
135-139	Humility – truth of self - brings us closer to God
140-145	God knows every little detail that lies within our hearts
146-149	Take care not to sit in judgment of others; that is God's responsibility
150-153	Faith in God will heal any human condition
154-158	God's "club" is open to all people
159-162	Through openness and humility we are best able to see Jesus Christ at work in our lives.
163-167	Christ's promise of peace and true safety
168-171	Presenting ourselves at the Lord's table just as we are
172-176	Be still and feel God's presence
177-180	Hunger after the really important things in life
181-186	Living within the boundary of God's love and protection
187-192	Transformation into true believers
193-198	No one except Jesus Christ has all the answers

199-203	We are never alone. Jesus Christ is always with us
204-207	Jesus travels with us even in the fiercest of storms
208-212	Keeping our eyes on the spiritual signposts in life
213-217	Be on red alert to challenges to our Christian values
218-220	The great high priest… or should I rather let us say our Lord's humble servant?
221-224	Our place in the great universe
225-228	Providing safe places for each other
229-233	Following the courage of our convictions
234-237	The power of prayer and hope for new beginnings
238-242	Opening our hearts to reveal the glory and love of God to others
243-246	God's gifts in the midst of chaos
247-251	Standing firm in one spirit with integrity
252-255	Staying connected to the community of the body of Christ
256-261	Turning your concerns over to God
262-265	Appendix 1 –references to Holy Scripture
266	Appendix 2 – about the author and illustrator

This book is dedicated to my Dad's younger brother, my Uncle Vernon, who died on April 13th, 2009, just prior to his 96th birthday. Vernon Augustus John Dolan was my trusted and dear friend for more than 60 years.

John Richard Dolan

Foreword

"The Mushroom Farm" is offered as nourishment for personal spiritual growth and to provide inspiration to you the reader.

Each story in the book stands alone, and is intended to provide strength, solace, comfort and reinforcement, particularly to Christians, as they experience similar events in their own lives.

The stories are my life experiences just as they happened and they are stories that have been used in sermons for more than fifteen years.

Each of my stories has been woven into Holy Scripture selected for that day. The cross referencing to scripture allows the reader the opportunity to explore their own stories in relation to God's word.

Through this sharing of experiences, the book's purpose is to offer hope and strength in troubled times and enhance one's joy in those special moments in life.

The stories selected for the "Mushroom Farm" follow my age in life. The stories travel through my early childhood in England and growing up in Llandaff, Wales.

They continue through my life studying and working in London and ultimately my life here in the United States, taking us through 52 stories to the present day...

The stories also contain the experience of a growing awareness of the Holy Spirit from more than fifteen years preaching experience as a Deacon, the combined effect of these timelines is to reveal a "forward movement" in my ability to discern the Divine in my life. I expect you, the reader to benefit greatly from discerning a similar "forward movement" in their own lives.

God is always present and available to us, but we as human beings have the opportunity for a growing discernment of that presence if, as Bishop Griswold describes it, "we just watch, listen and learn".

After reading "The Mushroom Farm", I expect you to relate my stories to your own spiritual journeys and be more sensitive to the presence of the Holy Spirit on your own journey through life...

Over the years I have listened very carefully to the responses to my sermon stories. The most common reaction from parishioners has been "you could have been talking about my own life and the issues I have had to face".

This has taught me that we are all living in the same world, subject to the same dangers and opportunities. It is how we cope and learn from our experiences that makes us different from each other. But we are fundamentally the same, and truly represent together the members of Christ's body here on earth.

Constructing this book has been a spiritual journey in itself; it has been a joy, and I am thankful for the privilege to have been able to complete it, and to make it available to those who read it.

John Richard Dolan

Acknowledgments

The concept for this book arose from the members of our congregation comparing my stories to their own lives. I was urged to put the stories into a format that can be shared with a larger audience. The loudest voice in this urging was my friend Cliff Egel, but there were many others… they know who they are.

Cliff introduced me to his son Paul, who had recently graduated from Long Beach State University, California. Thus began an enjoyable collaboration that has produced a set of outstanding illustrations that help bring life to the stories in this book.

I say thank you to my friends and other family members for their permission to be included in this book and for the "living material" that makes the book possible.

I am also so grateful to my family, particularly my wife Karen of thirty five years for her honest opinion of my work, her ideas and creativity and to our adult children Michelle and David for their support.

Thank you to members of the congregation at Emmanuel Episcopal Church, La Grange, Illinois and specifically to Louise Meyer, Linda Christiansen. Also to Rev. Don Frye and Kathy Burrows for their reality checks, and their early endorsement to the value of this project.

In the midst of the storm, God is with us

"... and they woke him up and said to him. Teacher, do you not care if we are perishing?"

The Sea of Galilee, on which today's gospel events took place, is a freshwater lake measuring at 14 miles, about the same length as Lake Geneva in Wisconsin, but about four times its width. The Sea of Galilee was the source of livelihood for at least four of Jesus' Disciples.

The lake, usually a quiet body of water, is surrounded by mountains except for a few areas to the south and northwest. Deep ravines cut into the mountains act as wind tunnels producing sudden and ferocious storms.

One can understand how fishermen in their flimsy wooden crafts reacted to the storms. The storms, appearing suddenly, as if out of nowhere were almost surreal, the work of the devil, intent on destroying their catch if not their lives.

But the disciples no longer had any reason to fear the lurking danger of storms. Now they had ironclad protection; Jesus would be their shield. But then, when exposed to the immediate physical dangers of a storm, how could their Jesus save them if he was sleeping at his post? They had to wake up Jesus, their insurance, their protector; they had to make certain that the Savior of the world did his job and saved them from the dangers of this world. This was Jesus' job, to protect them. Their following him and believing in him automatically bought them immunity from the troubles of the world.

Boy, did they miss the whole point of faith and their relationship with God through our Lord Jesus! And Jesus certainly let them know just how wrong they were. That it is Faith itself, the loving relationship with God through our Lord Jesus that supports us and equips us to cope with the inevitable problems that this life will bring.

My Grandmother, Lizzie Coyne, was a formidable lady who lived till 97 years of age and to my knowledge never saw a doctor. Nana, as we called her, lived in the town of Gosport near the British Royal Navy base at Portsmouth, England. Nana had five sisters, my great aunts, who owned and managed a well known, very large and very popular pub (an abbreviation I am sure at least some of you know for a public house, an establishment for the sale and consumption of alcoholic beverages). For the time I knew my great aunts I only remember ever seeing one great uncle, just one time. They were all sailors and all eventually died at sea in the Second World War. As a child I have no recollection of any mention ever made about the deaths of their husbands, except for just one time that I will describe in a few moments.

The six sisters had a morning routine that had to be seen to be believed. Every time I visited Nana I was witness to six ladies in long dresses and white aprons at 6 o'clock in the morning, rolling out huge, empty wooden beer barrels and replacing them with full ones, each weighing probably more than 200 pounds. Then with large wooden mallets they would hammer in bronze taps for that day's business. All this manual labor, with a war on; air raids by night, shortages, with loved ones dead or missing, and never a complaint or negative comment, at least never in the earshot of a three year old nephew and grandson. These six gentle ladies weren't raised to heave crates of beer bottles around and load trucks, but they got on and dealt with things; they coped.

One morning as Nana helped me get ready for our walk through the lanes to the pub, she said to me, "We have just heard that Auntie Doreen's husband, your Uncle Vance, who you saw home on leave just three months ago has been killed." (He, along with 800 shipmates, drowned when his ship was torpedoed.)

I remember sitting in the kitchen, hearing the normally placid Auntie Doreen crying out, "I do not deserve this. I have tried to live a good life; why should this happen to me? It is just not fair. How could God do this to me? I've gone to Church, and been good to others; it is just not fair. Where is God? I have prayed that he bring my Vance back to me and he hasn't. Jesus has deserted me. I work hard, I am kind to others, and I pull my weight. Why would God allow this to happen?"

Many of us have heard these words from those we love and cherish, or we have said these words ourselves. They are words that Job may have used in describing his frustrations with his life. They are difficult words to immediately respond to, especially when they are words from those who may be suffering or in great pain, situations where we just want our Lord Jesus to put his arms around us and take away the pain, to heal us and shield us from all dangers. How does our Lord Jesus respond to us in these situations?

When Jesus rebuked the wind in that fearsome storm on the Sea of Galilee, he did not promise those disciples there would be no more storms, but rather that he would be with them through whatever peril the storms brought them.

That is what Jesus promises us. He does not promise that if we believe in him, no evil will befall us, no crises, no tragedy will occur in our lives. What Jesus promises is that he will always be with us, loving us, supporting us, caring for us.

The power of God working through Jesus Christ rebuked the wind and calmed the storm. In the same way our faith in our Lord Jesus takes care of each one of us no matter what problems we face!

The essence of my Grandmother's response to my Auntie Doreen's cries echoed the words of Jesus to his disciples: "Doreen, it is the depth of your faith that will now carry you through this dreadful time." It is the firm belief that good will prevail over evil, that the creative, calming power of God works for us through our Lord Jesus. How do you think we can manage this place and the stress put on us and yet survive?

God does care for each of us. God loves us more than you can imagine. God is with us to soothe and nurture us. Even in the midst of this terrible war and in the depth of our personal grief, God is here with us and through Jesus Christ holds us and comforts us. Gentle Jesus strengthens us until, when the evil of the storm has passed, we are able to tell others of how Jesus was with us, how he loved us. How the depth and strength of our faith in Jesus received through our baptism will carry us through even the most terrible of times.

Gifts for those in need reveal his glory

"Then the wise men, opening their treasure chests, offered him gifts of Gold, Frankincense and Myrrh"

As a child I always loved the story of the birth of the Baby Jesus, our Lord and Savior Jesus born in the stable with the oxen and donkeys standing by.

The images of humility and simplicity struck me from an early age - the angelic face of Mary and the kind natured Joseph being so attentive to the newborn. But then a couple of days later we have the story of the three wise men, or were they Kings, or the strange word "Magi". Sometimes the three Kings seemed to arrive on the same day as Jesus was born. I never quite got the connection. Also what was the gifts thing all about? We all understand the gold… great… but frankincense and myrrh… what on earth were they? Also, was it more a question of two of the Kings forgetting their gifts, and so on their journey they stopped at the drugstore and picked up some perfume and deodorant as gifts... to make up for the gold or jewels that they had left behind.

A widely known kids' Christmas poem in Wales added to the confusion about the three wise men: "We three Kings of Orient are.....one on a bike and one in a car...one was walking forever talking...following yonder star".

Simply childhood musings? Or do some of us still retain some of the questions about the visit of the wise men or as with the Emperor's new clothes, do we never question the realities of the story?

The first clue to the real story is in the first verse of today's gospel, "wise men from the east". It is widely thought that the wise men were from Persia and thus they were Gentiles -a clear pointer that Christ's ministry was to be to the entire world and not just the Jewish community.

The word "wise men" first appeared in the King James translation. Scholars believe the original word Magi is from the Persian "Magus", a term referring to a priest sect who paid close attention to the position of the stars in the heavens. The Magis' names are thought in the Western Churches to be Caspar, Melchior and Balthazar.

As far as the gifts were concerned, as one scholar puts it, "They were gifts fit for God even more fitting than for an earthly King". Gold speaks for itself and was a symbol of Jesus' Kingship. Frankincense and Myrrh were not casual gifts; In the society at the time they were worth more than their weight in gold. Frankincense was widely valued both as medicine and in religious ceremony. Thus Frankincense is a symbol of Jesus holy priesthood. Myrrh was widely used as an embalming agent, and thus represented Jesus' suffering that would take place in his life.

Of course there are many legends and theories about who the wise men really were, and the nature of the gifts. Some even believe that the gold was stolen by one of the thieves that was ultimately crucified alongside our Lord.

I believe one of the most important points for us in these times is that the wise men acted selflessly in travelling long distances and offered meaningful gifts to the newborn Jesus, without expecting a return on their investment.

In the early part of the 1900's, my great Grandmother ran a public house near the Portsmouth naval base, in southern England. The drinking establishment was frequented by many sailors from the naval base and became a very busy and successful business. The pub remained in the family until well into the 1950s.

The Pub's name was "The Old House at Home" and my grandmother and her five sisters all worked as barmaids and cooks at the pub. I can remember as a small child helping Nana (my Grandmother) roll out the empty beer barrels at 6 o'clock in the morning. Boy, those sailors drank a lot of beer.

In the 1920's great poverty existed in the town where the Pub was situated. It is hard for us to believe now, but many kids had no shoes on their feet, and the children were lucky if they received one meal a day.

Nana told me that every day my great grandmother would cook five extra meat or chicken pies, and when they came out of the oven she would place them outside on the kitchen window sills. She would then conveniently forget they were there until the following day. The following day when she placed five new steaming hot pies on the window sills, five empty, clean dishes were there from the previous days.

No one ever knew which families were fed by those pies or how many children from the village went to bed with food in their stomachs rather than going hungry, and nothing was ever spoken about those acts of kindness by my great grandma. That went on for many years.

In our Gospel story today, I believe that the wise men led the way in offering their gifts of Gold, Frankincense and Myrrh to the Christ child. We follow their example in our gifts of love and kindness to each other. The gift of visits to the sick in the hospital, the outstretched hand to those in financial trouble. Our contribution here in La Grange through organizations such as 'BEDS', our local homeless shelter, and our outreach work in Sudan.

We need to continue to dig deep and change our priorities, if necessary, so that we can meet our financial pledge to our Lord Jesus.

Individually we all need to bake extra pies and leave them on our window sills for those in greater need than ourselves. We all need to live our lives by giving without expecting something in return.

If we give from our hearts, in the smallest of ways, we will receive more than we ever can imagine.

Turning over the stress of living to Jesus Christ

From St. John's Gospel: "Zeal for your house will consume me"

I think it fair to say that we all live stress-filled lives, sometimes to the point of the stress being overwhelming. Stress related to our work and our family responsibilities. Stress from money or health issues. Stress related to retirement and finding new roles for us in our lives. Stress when we have lost control on issues, and stress because we have made bad choices or simply made mistakes in our lives. Stress from addictions and most of all stress from sinful desires and actions that interfere with our relationship with God.

In my opinion, this extract from John's Gospel is one of the very few documented occasions when stress got to our Lord. He became angry at the moneylenders in the temple profiteering from the sale of animals and birds for sacrifice, and turning the temple into a marketplace. Jesus told those who were selling the doves, "Take these things out of here! Stop making my Father's house a marketplace!"

The season of Lent is the time for us to reexamine our priorities, and how we conduct business, the business of running our lives. It is a time for us to examine the basics of our relationship with Jesus Christ. To reexamine what is important to us and to our relationship with God. It is time for us to take the busyness and distractions in our lives and get them out of here… so we can concentrate on the important things.

My Dad, Walter Dolan, characterized the distractions in our lives as spiders in our closets. We all have them, but spiders are very adept at hiding from us; creeping into the crevices in our hearts. Thus we need to do a thorough cleaning job and move the clutter in our lives out of our living space. The living space has to be available to be filled with the presence of the Holy Spirit. And Lent is the special time to do this cleaning job.

When I was growing up in Wales, my Dad was an electrical engineer by profession. One day in early 1952, Dad brought home the plans to build our first television set. This would be the first TV on our block, and the plan was to have it completed in time for the Coronation of Queen

Elizabeth the second in June of that year. My Dad said it would be a wonderful experience for the whole family to work on a project together. Having a television would also open up a whole new world for us. It really did sound exciting.

In John's Gospel, did Jesus lose his temper because the cheating was being done on holy ground? Or did Jesus lose his temper because the poor were being extorted in the name of religion? Take your pick. Either way it was a highly stressful situation.

To Jesus, taking advantage of people in need was as bad if it occurred in the street or in the Temple. It didn't matter whether the offender was a tax collector or a Temple priest. Jesus took his whip to the crooks in the Temple to make a simple point.

The Temple would be destroyed because those who controlled the religion of Israel had betrayed the people, the nation, and the nation's God…and they had piled on abuse and stress on people who were already looking for forgiveness.

Back in the Dolan's dining room: the television project was OK for the first couple of months; then it gradually began to take over our lives. I can still remember the odor of the burning solder, and the melting plastic of the homemade electronic components.

And then another stress was added: my mother, unbeknownst to my Dad, had sent out invitations to just about everyone on the block to watch the coronation on our new television. Invitations had been sent out to view an event on our new television, which at that point of time was simply an array of untested electrical components, sitting on our dining room table.

The irony of today's Gospel story is that ordinary folk, realizing they had broken God's law, sought to approach God with a sacrifice, in order to atone. They were then being cheated at the very point or place in their life where they were most under stress, and most needing to be nurtured. Rather than merely reforming the system, rapping the abusers on their knuckles and telling the priests and their assistants to do better, Jesus called down judgment on them. A new Temple would be created, a temple made not of stone but of human beings, a temple open to all and for all.

The Queen's Coronation was scheduled for Tuesday, June 2nd, 1952. As of the previous Friday, some components of the Dolan's TV had been tested individually, but there had not been even one test of the whole contraption. You can just imagine the stress in our home. I will always remember my Mom saying, "I will never be able to show my face again to our neighbors. How can they watch the Coronation with that hotchpotch of electrical stuff? This darn television has become a monster in our house!"

Well, the first test of the complete television was scheduled for Saturday morning, three days before the coronation.

In the Temple, the persons selling the sacrificial animals undoubtedly overpriced their goods and the moneylenders overcharged their commissions. Sounds only too familiar to many modern day experiences. But for those people looking for atonement and forgiveness this aggravation just increased the stress in their lives, it made matters worse for them.

Our Lord Jesus would have none of this. He would destroy the temple and raise it again in three days. His disciples had recalled that it had been written in Psalm 69 verse 9, *"For zeal for thy house has consumed me."*

But of course what the disciples did not understand was that when Jesus was describing the destruction and rebuilding of the temple in three days, He was talking about his own passion and resurrection, the creation of an entirely new kingdom.

On the Saturday morning, the television components were linked together, some worked, and some didn't. The stress in the Dolan household grew even worse, to the point where my Mum was not speaking to Dad.

Then by mid afternoon we had a picture. It was the proper size, but it was a negative picture - black where white should be, and white where black should be. Further, the picture was upside down and back to front. Nevertheless, it worked. The stress eased and after numerous adjustments we had a proper picture.

The electrical components were then assembled inside a

prebuilt television cabinet, and we were all set for a dress rehearsal television showing on Sunday after Church. Remember the Queen's Coronation then was only two days away.

In today's Gospel story, what was it that tipped the scale to make Jesus so angry and that created such a stressful situation?

I believe quite simply it was the temple, this holy place, looking just like the marketplace. What should have been a model of another way of living and of relating to one another, an example of God's way, had become no different from the way of the world. The model of God had become the mimic of man.

In the late afternoon of the Sunday, (after two more hours of Dad's adjustments, and two more hours of my Mum saying to Dad, "Stop fiddling with it! You will mess it up! Leave well alone!"), we turned on the television. It worked perfectly. Hurrah.

On Monday evening, after Dad returned from work (now just 15 hours before the coronation was due to be televised) we turned on the TV. I noticed right away the picture was smaller in size. Dad denied it,,, and said it was fine. However, gradually over the space of two hours the picture got smaller and smaller and smaller so that it was no bigger than a matchbox.

You can imagine the reaction. I thought my Mother was going to emulate Jesus, beat my Dad and throw the television out in the garbage; but cooler heads prevailed.

One of us came up with an idea. On Tuesday morning we would purchase a large magnifying lens, which we would then attach to the television screen! The Dolan family and all our neighbors will then be able to watch the coronation in fine style.

That is exactly what happened and we had a great day. Success all round!!

The experience of making the television did have some good points to it, but the project took over our home. The project brought out stress, and strained relations in our family. The project was a distraction from other things we could have done together as a family, and it turned our family home into, if not a marketplace, then more like a zoo of electronic equipment.

By the way, the day after the coronation, my Dad put his television into the attic where it remained for the rest of his life. The following weekend he went out and purchased a commercially available television set.

The zeal for the television project in our family home really did nearly consume us.

Let us turn over to God the stress in our lives by committing ourselves to an even stronger loving relationship with Jesus Christ.

The relationship between faith and God's mercy

"Jesus said to the Canaanite woman, 'Great is your faith! Let it be done for you as you wish.' And her daughter was healed instantly."

Two clear themes thread their way through today's lessons. There is the theme of God's mercy: from the Book of Isaiah to the Psalms to St. Paul's letter to the Romans we hear the offering of mercy and compassion by God for His children.

The second theme we hear is of the promise of a new life. The Canaanite woman and her daughter's terrible suffering have ended. Jesus' healing provides them the promise of a new life, a life free of pain and struggle, the anguish replaced with love and peace through our Lord Jesus Christ.

Let us describe the context of today's gospel. Jesus has traveled outside of the Jewish world to the districts of Tyre and Sidon. Jesus understood that God's circle and plan extends to the whole world, so he was willing to take his teachings to the north to Phoenicia, the land of the Canaanites.

But Jesus was raised as a Jew, and to the Jews two thousand years ago, the word "Canaanite" was synonymous with pagan. If you were a Jew you simply did not go within a mile of any known Canaanite; and both Jesus and the Canaanite woman were obviously aware of that.

To approach a Jew as she did, the Canaanite mother must have been desperate, probably at her wits' end; and our Lord's initial response to the woman echoed the bias that is described to us as part of his Jewish culture. In the words from today's Gospel, "It is not fair to take the children's food and throw it to the dogs." Jesus is admitting to his own people's attitude toward that pagan community.

But then the situation was transformed: whether it was divine inspiration or merely the act of a loving, committed mother, whatever the rationale, the Canaanite woman would simply not give up. She persisted to make certain she received Jesus' attention, and she was not disappointed.

Jesus Christ, the Son of David, Jesus Christ our Lord and Savior showed the great extent of His mercy and compassion, and through the mother's faith, healed the daughter.

Growing up in Wales in the 1950s I suffered from asthma. When I was twelve years old, I spent about one week a month bedridden, and the disease prevented me from pursuing many of my childhood sports and interests.

This was a difficult time for my family and me. There was virtually no medication available at that time for asthma sufferers, no ventihalers or medicine to relieve the sense of suffocation that accompanied a bad attack. There was a deteriorating nature to the disease of asthma, and emotionally, as I am sure with many families, we had a great struggle to deal with the symptoms. My mother in her love would become particularly desperate.

But then one day we heard about a certain Dr. Rhys Evans, a nationally noted asthma specialist, who had recently arrived in Wales from a research hospital in London.

The key to today's Gospel lies in the words, *"Woman, great is your faith! Let it be done for you as you wish."* It is her faith that makes all the difference. We heard in last week's Gospel, a situation where Jesus' own disciples showed little faith. Peter took the rap, but I didn't notice any of the other disciples rushing to volunteer in his place to step out onto the Sea of Galilee.

Here we have this pagan, this Canaanite woman, showing greater faith than Jesus' own disciples. And the Canaanite woman's faith was rewarded.

Some of you may know that in Wales there are many

persons with the same name. It is not uncommon to find a whole village composed of Davises, Evanses, Joneses, Thomases and Williamses. The way round that is to attach a trade or occupation to the name, thus Evans the Butcher, Jones the Rector, Thomas the pub.

Dr. Rhys Evans soon had his label. In our village Dr. Evans became known as "Evans the Quack". Now I must tell you that in Wales "Quack" is not in any way a derogatory term, I remember it just as a friendly reference to a medical doctor.

My mother arranged a visit for me with Dr. Evans; good old National Health Service. I remember even in those days, we had to wait about six weeks for an appointment. Evans the Quack had a large intimidating office. I remember him as a man of small stature, with rimless spectacles and a very serious disposition.

As things usually happen, I was of course as fit as a fiddle on the day of the office visit, and I remember feelings of fraud and embarrassment having to be there. But my Mom persisted in our going to see him.

"Mrs. Dolan," he said, "thank you for bringing John here to see me. I will do whatever I can to make life easier for you." Dr. Evans went on, "I have seen much suffering with this roguish disease called asthma," but then his face broke into a broad smile.

He said, "I am glad to be able to tell you that there are medicines being developed that will help your son John a great deal in his life."

We left Dr. Evans with mixed feelings. My Mom had faith that this visit was different. I saw it as one more medical setting, one more doctor with nothing to show for it, except the ever present dread of the next asthma attack with no medication.

Today's Gospel shouts out to us the importance of faith in our lives. The Canaanite woman claims her place in the Kingdom based on faith.

Of course the Kingdom of God depends on exactly this kind of faith, rather than on any nationalistic, cultural or family of origin. *"Have mercy on me, Lord, Son of David,"* was the cry from this pagan woman whose prayer was heard and whose faith was rewarded.

Back in Wales, the next asthma attack came almost as if it had its own cruel schedule. My Mother said, "I am going to call Dr. Evans if it gets any worse."

My recollection is that my dad and I responded in a manner very different from my Mother's: "Dr. Evans can't do anything; why bother him? Anyway he is much too busy to have time for us... what good would it do anyway?"

My mother persisted, and got in contact with Dr. Evans; and the asthma did get much worse.

Sometime later I remember a knock on my bedroom door, and Dr. Rhys Evans walked in. He sat down on the edge of the bed and he put his arm round me, and he took a small round pill box out of his briefcase. Dr. Evans smiled at me, and I remember him saying, " John, I have something in this box that will change your life."

In the box was one small pill, "prednisone", a steroid derivative used to this day.

In twenty minutes the asthma attack subsided, and from that day the fear of asthma was removed from our lives. Five years later I was strong, fit and healthy, albeit probably a hundred pounds heavier. I was in a rowing crew competing on the Thames River in London, which is a story for another day.

My mother, through her faith and persistence, together with Dr. Evans' mercy and compassion, changed the world for me, and provided the promise of better days for our family, just as Jesus changed the world for the Canaanite woman and her daughter.

Thank you, Joan Dolan, thank you Dr. Rhys Evans, "Evans the Quack!" But most of all, thank you to our loving and compassionate God.

In the words of the prayer from the Canaanite woman: *Lord Jesus Christ, Son of David, Son of the Living God, have mercy on us.*

We are all equal in God's eyes

From today's reading from the Gospel according to St. Luke, "For all who exalt themselves will be humbled, but all who humble themselves will be exalted."

I love this part of Luke's Gospel. Jesus is right in the midst of community; he is right here immersed with us, experiencing all our human strengths and weaknesses. Throughout scripture we read of Christ's reactions to different people in community; and we find great comfort because we gradually understand that Jesus was truly one of us, a human being in every respect with a clear understanding of who we are and the blessings and challenges that we all face in this life.

Jesus has previously taught us that God is always there for us, but we need to be diligent in our prayers and listen very carefully for God's response.

Jesus now encounters the self-righteous among us, those people - and we all know them - the people who make it very difficult for us not to be judgmental. Jesus tells the parable of the Pharisee and the tax Collector. He describes their relative positions in society, but how the Pharisee who should have known better, behaved in an unacceptable self- righteous manner - behavior, I might add, that in our own lives I am sure we have all encountered and we can all relate to.

As a random and totally outrageous thought, maybe I can remember self-righteousness even in my own behavior; years ago of course…I am way past that now!

When I was growing up in the Cathedral Parish of Llandaff in South Wales, we had a particularly strong sense of village community because we were constantly engaged as a community in rebuilding our beloved Cathedral.

In the words of the Cathedral website, "On the evening of January 2, 1941 during World War II a German bomb had fallen beside the cathedral, causing massive destruction including that of the organ. Of British cathedrals, only Coventry Cathedral was damaged more. Major restorations and reconfigurations were carried out in the 1950s and the building was back in use by June 1958."

During the 1950s, our services were mostly held in the

Lady Chapel. I am told attendance was even higher than prewar, and we were all jammed together into the relatively small space the chapel provided. Every Sunday we sat in the same rows. In our row were the Dolans; Wyndham Thomas, a shopkeeper in the village; Mrs. Jill Brooke, a friend of my Mum's; and two other families.

Jammed together in the Lady Chapel, almost sitting on each other's laps, was inconvenient, but it was also intimate. It was nurturing and we were all on a sense of mission together. As one, we were determined to rebuild our great Cathedral. We were unpretentious and unassuming, just ourselves looking forward each week to being together on a Sunday morning. We were welcoming and enjoyed each other in a way that I have not experienced since.

You hear stories of the people sheltering in the London Underground during the blitz…the feelings of closeness were probably similar to those we felt in the Lady Chapel in Llandaff Cathedral.

In Luke's Gospel, Jesus was generous to the Tax Collector. He knew full well that the Tax Collector was an agent of Rome, the occupier of Israel. He knew this man was in fact a collaborator with the enemy, but he also saw his repentance and his humility.

I believe Jesus understood that the Pharisee probably lived a moral, spirit-filled life and carried out his social responsibilities to the best of his ability, including tithing to his Church.

But the Pharisee also appeared self-righteous: "Look at me, I'm the righteous one. I am not like other people - thieves, rogues or even like this tax collector."

It is very clear that Our Lord was not at all impressed with the Pharisee's behavior. However gifted he was, however disciplined and moral his code of life was, the Pharisee was self-righteous and judgmental.

Back in Llandaff, one glorious Sunday morning the great temporary wall between the Lady Chapel and the Sanctuary had gone, and there was this vast space in which to hold our Liturgy.

We had all entered through the normal Chapel side door, and there for the first time we saw the High Altar, the beautiful new choir area, the nave...oh my...oh my. But then our thoughts turned to more mundane issues: where would we sit? Would our tight little row of persons still sit together? No way. My Dad's family had always sat in the third row on the Gospel side, and that was our domain from then on until Dad died some twenty five years later. Jill Brooke sat hidden away at the back of the choir stalls, in the seat closest to the Lady Chapel. The other families in our Lady Chapel row were scattered around the Cathedral, and Wyndham Thomas, our friend, the somewhat portly, friendly gentleman, was nowhere to be seen.

Some commentaries I have read are more generous toward the Pharisee in today's Gospel story than perhaps I am. I, of course, agree that living a moral and spiritual life is important. To use your God-given gifts to the maximum is clearly important. To give generously and where possible tithe to your Church is not just important; it is essential. But also essential is how you present yourself, your God-given gifts, particularly your faith, to other people in your life.

We are all equal in God's eyes, and we should be reminded of this when we present ourselves to our fellow human beings. The words in Luke's Gospel are very clear and unambiguous to me. Jesus said, "*I tell you, this man* (the tax collector) *went down to his home justified... rather than the other*" (the Pharisee).

The second week in our new home in the Chancel at Llandaff Cathedral, the Dolan family, having arrived as usual incredibly early, were sitting alone, third row from the front. Suddenly we see this familiar, rather large figure, Wyndham Thomas, but Mr. Thomas is now dressed in a black vestment with a silver cross round his neck, with his hands together as if in prayer. As he passed our row, Mr. Thomas turned to my Dad and bowed his head. My Dad turned to me and said quietly, "I always thought this grandiose Cathedral thing would go to Wyndham's head. He just can't control his need to show the world how pious he is, and how well he fits into this beautiful building."

In due course we found out that Wyndham Thomas had appointed himself as an unofficial sub-deacon, and he was to continue to parade around the Church until a new Dean arrived who promptly stopped the behavior; and I believe Wyndham Thomas joined another Church.

We remained firm friends, but we never had the opportunity to speak to Jill Brooke again during Church. She would slip in and out of the old Chapel door. To this day, I believe, she still sits in the back row of the choir, out of sight but perhaps close to her memories of our time of being equal, of being humble and spiritually focused, in the good times, when we were all equal, all crowded together in that tiny Lady Chapel.

The good news from today's Gospel is that we are all equal in the eyes of God's love. There is no need for exaggerated physical signs of piety. God loves us all equally regardless of what we feel about each other, or how we feel about ourselves.

I have heard it said that the ground at the foot of the Cross of Christ at Calvary is level, dead level. In the same way the resurrected Christ reaches out to all of us as equals.

God loves us all with a passion that is beyond anything we can experience in this life... what a wonderful gift.

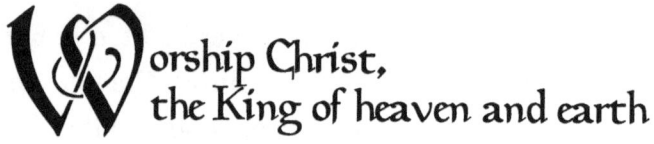 orship Christ, the King of heaven and earth

From the book of the Revelation of St. John the Divine," To Him who loves us and freed us from our sins by his blood, and made us to be a kingdom, ... to him be glory and dominion forever and ever. Amen."

This Sunday is often known as the Sunday of Christ the King. Today, in a sense, we come to the end of our journey through the story of Jesus on this earth. But we know that with Jesus there is no end; we are simply at the end of a cycle and next week, the first Sunday of Advent of course, we start our journey with Jesus all over again.

The Festival of Christ the King has not been around for very long. As recently as 1925 the Franciscans persuaded Pope Pius XI to establish it as a Roman Catholic Feast day on the last Sunday in October, mainly as a counterpart to the Protestant emphasis on a "Reformation Sunday" on that date. Vatican Two, in 1969, then moved Christ the King day to the last Sunday in the Christian year. Now virtually all Christian denominations celebrate Christ the King on the last Sunday of the Church year. What started seventy five years ago as an expression of divisiveness in the Church now presents itself as a symbol of Christian unity, the symbol of Christ the King.

When I grew up in post war Britain, the monarchy, the house

of Windsor, was at the absolute height of its popularity. "Annus horribilis" and scandal were unthinkable in those days, and if there was a sniff of scandal, no newspaper would ever take the risk of publishing it. King George the sixth and his Queen Elizabeth (now the hundred year old Queen mother) were a source of hope and inspiration during World War II. The beautiful young Queen Elizabeth the second just added to the public acclaim.

The Queen's coronation in 1952 was quite magnificent. We built miniature coronation coaches in school, painted with gold leaf paint I might add, we had banners and other decorations strung across the street, we had fireworks and block parties. As a teenager in Wales I remember very clearly the public's love and devotion to their new Queen. I truly believe some people felt that our Queen was a little closer to God than a mere human being. For the British people, who had been deprived even basic foodstuffs for many long years during, and after the war, for a people whose nation had been bankrupted by their long war against Hitler's evil, the monarchy became the symbol of hope and salvation.

In 1957, just five years after the coronation, it was announced that the Queen was coming to my home town, Cardiff, Wales, to dedicate our newly restored Llandaff Cathedral. The thousand-year-old Cathedral was virtually destroyed by a German bomb in 1944. It was my parish church; it is where I served as an acolyte and where I still have strong connections.

In 1957, I was a second year torchbearer and when the schedule came out, I was to be in the procession for the Queen's visit. I could not believe it: I would see the Queen!

Today's Old Testament readings highlight the historic hope of the people of Israel: to live under the divine and just rule of God. The longing to have once again a King like David, the ideal King, beloved of God. And during the time of Jesus, the Jewish people continued this longing to have a strong King who would ease their hard life under the Roman occupation and give them back their independence.

Jesus knew what the Jewish people expected, but he knew who he was, that his realm, his Kingdom, is not from this world; that rather than being a King in this world, he is the King of Kings, the Lord of Lords.

God intervened in the life of the Jewish people, but not in the way anyone imagined. The Kingship of Christ lay not in pomp and ceremony nor in great armies, but in his victory over death. The ultimate sacrifice of Jesus' life for us and his resurrection gives us all the greatest of all gifts, that of life eternal.

I remember being so excited at the Queen's visit and the dedication service that was planned, that I felt physically sick. During the service itself, I don't know how I kept the torch upright.

Twelve state trumpeters announced our procession as we entered the Cathedral. Courtiers and Lord Marshals with their plumed hats, local dignitaries, Lord Lieutenants of the counties, Beefeaters, they were all there in the procession. The Archbishop of Wales and other Bishops, clerics. My memory is that I just looked straight ahead, following the whispered instruction from the Master of Ceremonies behind me.

About six of us acolytes sat down in our assigned seats close to the choir. The music was extraordinary; the atmosphere was electric. Our Queen was here in our Cathedral. Then suddenly I saw the Queen and the Duke of Edinburgh. Not only did I just see them, they sat down directly opposite us. It felt like a dream and I remember wondering if we were worshipping her or God, or was she partly God.

Then the service started; I clearly remember the point in the service when the Dean of the Cathedral said, in his familiar voice, "Let us pray." I saw the Queen solemnly kneel down and pray with us like any other human being. The separation of earthly and heavenly kingdoms was right there in front of me: Her Britannic Majesty, Elizabeth, Queen of the United Kingdom and the British Commonwealth, was together with us, praying and worshipping, worshipping the real King, the King of Kings, the Prince of Peace.

Kings in history were absolute rulers. They attained earthly power by raising and leading armies into war against other countries. Jesus the King has also raised an army, an army of those faithful to him. Jesus fights a war, a war against sin and death, a war against the power and influence of the evil

one. But through his death and Resurrection, Jesus has won the war against evil.

In modern days, the pomp and circumstance, so much in evidence that morning at Llandaff Cathedral still surrounds the Monarch, but with all its grandeur it is nothing compared with the praise and glory we offer to the real King. Just as Queen Elizabeth kneeled in homage to Christ the King, so we offer all praise and honor, and we offer ourselves to His service. As Christians, Kingship is a simple issue. All that we are asked to do is to accept that Jesus fought and won the war for our sakes and for us to recognize him as the King of Kings.

One of my favorite hymns growing up is number 399 in our hymnal: *"Oh worship the King all glorious above! O gratefully we sing his power and his love! Our shield and defender, the Ancient of days, pavilioned in splendor and girded with praise."* These words took on a new meaning for me after I experienced our Queen Elizabeth in silent prayer, worshipping the King of Kings, Jesus our Lord and savior.

On Christ the King Sunday, Christians recognize and worship Christ as King of heaven and earth, a loving and compassionate King, a King for all time without challenge and without end. To our Lord Jesus Christ be all glory and honor forever and ever.

You also should do as I have done to you

"Our Lord Jesus said to his disciples, 'For I have set you an example, that you also should do as I have done to you.'"

The night before the feast of the Passover, Jesus gathered with his friends, his faithful disciples. Jesus knew that the end was near, and he was to show his disciples an act of humility that we have reenacted here this evening, two thousand years later.

The Son of God, their master and Rabbi, their teacher, was to show his disciples how they were to behave to others in the world. Through the foot washing, Jesus was to demonstrate through the most menial of tasks, how much he loved his disciples and how they were to behave to others in the world.

In preparing for this sermon, I searched my heart to identify those people in my life who have really washed my feet.

My uncle, Vernon Dolan, will be 96 years old a week from today, April 9th, 2009. He is now physically frail. He lies in a hospital bed in Wales near his home two blocks from where I was raised. He is being cared for in the same hospital as his wife, my dear Aunt Jenny.

Uncle Vernon is my dad's younger brother; and he has not just been my uncle, he has been my friend for more than sixty years. He has been there for me whenever I have needed him. Similarly I have tried to emulate that behavior and be there for him.

The night before Jesus was betrayed, as they gathered in that Upper Room, they were there to commemorate the exodus of God's people Israel from their slavery under Pharaoh. It was the Lord's Passover. God had given elaborate instructions to His people for the preparation of this feast. The entrée was lamb, but not any ordinary lamb—a lamb without blemish or defect.

Every time they ate that meal, the Israelites ate it in remembrance of the Lord and His mercy. It was a meal full of hope and promise, but hope and promise under the very threat of death. That first night in Egypt, when God set His people free, it was in the midst of imminent danger. In every household in Egypt the firstborn of man and beast would die, except where the blood of a sacrificial lamb marked the door. At those houses the deadly plague passed over, sparing all within.

Uncle Vernon was a thirty year career officer in the British Royal Navy. He retired as Commander Dolan, Executive officer on the Aircraft Carrier HMS Indefatigable.

I remember uncle Vernon as a tall, almost intimidating individual. He was always very proper, and if one arranged to meet him somewhere at a particular time, then no matter if you travelled one block or four thousand miles, you were expected to be there on time.

As a child I would see uncle Vernon when he was on shore leave; and he might be gone more than six months at a time; in the China Sea one moment, San Diego and Hawaii the next. On one of his visits, he and I were talking about my love of the Boy Scouts, and I asked him would he be available to be the judge in our annual knot tying competition, which was coming up in about six months. He consulted his schedule and agreed to do it.

As the months went by, I would ask my mom and dad about uncle Vernon's whereabouts. When asked whether they thought uncle Vernon would remember the knot-tying. Their reply was, "Good gracious, John, Uncle Vernon is engaged in the Korean war in the Far East! Are you being serious?"

On the night of their deliverance, God's people Israel ate that first Passover with mixed emotions: with gratitude and joy, to be sure, but tinged with dread—for the angel of death was passing overhead. Imagine a banquet given in your honor, but with live ammunition whizzing over your head. These people knew they had received mercy; they had been miraculously delivered from sure and certain death.

This, then, was Israel's Passover, the Old Testament sacramental meal of deliverance. In that meal, God's people dined on the body of the very animal that gave them life by dying in their place. It was a communion of sorts—a communion in the body that died to save.

On the night of the knot tying competition, I had not heard anything from uncle Vernon. But in the hope of his coming, I stood staring out of the window looking toward the railway station.

I must have been there for about two hours with my mom trying to distract me to other things and making excuses for uncle Vernon; and then, right on time, I saw this tall figure striding up the road, in full Royal Navy dress uniform. I can still visualize the gold on his sleeves and cap. He knocked on the door, I answered it and he said, "Mr. John Dolan?" I said, "Yes." He said, "Commander Vernon Dolan reporting for duty."

Uncle Vernon truly washed my feet that night; I will never forget it. I took great heart that night when my uncle Vernon travelled thousands of miles to meet his commitment to his nine year old nephew.

So similarly take heart this night. Death and destruction may loom and lurk on every side, but everything that troubles us and all that potentially robs us of our joy is eclipsed tonight in this banquet feast of love demonstrated particularly in our foot washing.

"For I have set you an example, that you also should do as I have done to you."

Fast forward close to twenty years from the time of the knot tying competition. November 3rd, 1970: I was unpacking my suitcase in a hotel on Michigan Avenue in Chicago. I was committed to a year's contract with my employer in Chicago; and the first reality of what I had done was hitting me hard.

I would not see my parents and family for at least a year; I knew nobody. Was this all a great mistake? Then the phone rang. I answered it and a voice said, "This is uncle Vernon. John, I just want you to know what a great adventure you have started; and if you need anything I am here."

To this day I have no idea how uncle Vernon found what hotel I was staying at, but I do know he washed my feet for a second time that evening and I have never forgotten it.

"For I have set you an example, that you also should do as I have done to you."

God bless and protect uncle Vernon and aunt Jenny. God Bless us all and all our loved ones as we travel through this night toward the inevitable death of our Lord Jesus tomorrow.

Dedicated to Vernon Augustus John Dolan died April 13, 2009

God's love transcends all human conditions

"...For he knew who was to betray him; for this reason he said, 'Not all of you are clean.'"

The word 'betrayal' is defined in the dictionary as "the act of desertion, the act of abandonment." Betrayal has to be one of the most personal, one of the most hurtful of acts that can be perpetrated by one human being against another. Betrayal, particularly by one you love, and who professes to love you, is surely one of the most traumatic experiences of life in this world. Being betrayed leaves deep personal wounds, wounds that are difficult to heal, wounds that even if they do heal, frequently leave severe scars for the rest of one's life.

In John's Gospel this evening we hear of the most infamous of betrayals, how Judas abandoned the love of our Lord Jesus. We also hear how Jesus, even though he knew of the betrayal, responded with an act of love, by washing the feet of Judas along with all the other disciples. I have shared experiences before about my childhood growing up in Cardiff, Wales. In the early fifties there were very few Jewish children in Cardiff High School. There were probably fewer than a dozen out of 800 enrolled students.

One of these Jewish students was Andrew Weinberg, and Andrew was a friend of mine. Andrew was different from other kids at school: he ate different foods, he took off on different holidays, and he didn't come to morning prayers at the Assembly hall. He had always come round to play on Sunday morning, but he also was the only kid I knew that didn't have a dad at home.

I asked him one day where his dad was. He replied simply, " My mum says that one day shortly before we left our home in Austria to move to Britain, that my dad just got up one morning and left us. He quit on us, John, he abandoned my mum and me. It makes me so angry and so lonely. How could he do it to us? We loved him and I thought he loved us. I tell you John, one day I will find him and I will hurt him like he hurt my mum and me."

I remember that he made a fist and punched at an invisible enemy. I was sad for Andrew, but the look in his eyes at that moment made me afraid for him.

In thinking about Jesus' reaction to the betrayal by Judas, the human feelings experienced by Jesus were undoubtedly very much the same as Andrew Weinberg's, but Jesus' words and actions were quite different. Even possessed with the knowledge that Judas, one of his beloved disciples, had betrayed him, this did not distract or deter Jesus from his act of love to all his disciples. He washed the feet of his disciples to show them that in the same way that their Lord and teacher could humble himself before them in an act of love, they in turn must show the love of our Father in heaven to all people in this world, regardless of peoples' actions or words, regardless of race or creed. Jesus reflected the unconditional love of God for all people for all time. How did Andrew Weinberg deal with his feelings of the betrayal by his Dad?

Andrew's story takes a different turn. It was only in the early fifties, in postwar Britain, that the public started hearing the details about Auschwitz and the Nazi death camps. Lord Russell of Liverpool had written a book as a full public expose of what horrors had occurred under the Nazis.

For whatever good reason Andrew's mum had decided to keep the truth from the young Andrew. Andrew's dad did not get up and leave his home voluntarily that morning. He did not quit on his family. He, along with millions of other Jews, was forced from his home at gunpoint, never to be seen again.

Years later I know Andrew eventually, possessed of the truth, was able to grieve the death of his dad. And the true betrayal that Andrew had to come to terms with, was not by his dad, but the betrayal of humanity by the ideals of Nazism.

We know how Jesus felt when betrayed by Judas because Jesus was a human being in every way. However, despite the hurt, despite all the normal human reactions to this grievous act by Judas, Jesus was still able to display his love by washing the feet of Judas.

Jesus, as a human being, in dealing with his human emotions in reaction to the betrayal and still being able to show his love for Judas, was reflecting the unconditional love of God for us all, now and forever. God's love is a love that transcends all human conditions, all human actions or words. God is there for us, waiting for us, loving us all, now and for evermore.

Growth through love and obedience

"I am the vine, you are the branches. Those who abide in me and I in them bear much fruit, because apart from me you can do nothing."

A group of us are privileged to share a mid-week Bible study Group, and we are now within six chapters of the end of the sixty-six chapters of the book of Isaiah. Our journey through Isaiah has been a marathon of oracles, predictions and reflections. The journey has been rich and rewarding, but it has been arduous, and the clarity of today's Gospel stands in wonderful contrast.

Today's story of the vine and the branches has always been one of my favorites, but as I read it this week, John's Gospel is like a refreshing oasis in the hot deserted landscape of a hostile desert. The difficult, sometimes vague, sometimes for me chaotic, perceptions of

God as expressed in Isaiah are overlaid in my mind by the fulfilled, focused and clear words of Jesus.

Jesus tells us that God the father is the gardener, that he, Jesus, is the vine, and that we are the branches. The branches have every opportunity to produce spiritual fruit from their lives but it all depends on creating and maintaining a loving, committed, obedient relationship between the branches and the vine. Human beings cannot flourish and prosper alone, and branches that do not have the life giving relationship with God will perish.

When I was fifteen, growing up in Cardiff, Wales, my friend Mac and I decided we were going into the mushroom growing business. We had seen an advertisement in a magazine – a commercial mushroom-growing company would provide all the materials: mushroom seeds (known as spores to us in the business), compost substance that the mushrooms would grow well in, and trays for them to grow in. All we needed was a warm, dark place. Then, when we had a bumper crop of mushrooms, the mushroom company would guarantee to buy them at a pre-established price per pound. This was, put in modern American terminology, a "slam dunk guaranteed success".

The Apostle John most likely wrote his Gospel from Ephesus in modern-day Turkey around 90 AD to the church, which included both Jews and Gentiles. In his teachings Jesus was particularly skillful at using terminology that was both familiar and comfortable to his audiences whether they be Jew or Gentile. For example the Old Testament contains many references to the vine motif, which was a well-known symbol for the nation of

Israel. Usually when it was referring to Israel, scripture does so with negative connotations because Israel did not produce good fruit as a vine. Isaiah 5, for example, tells of how God planted and cared for the vine. However, when He looked for good grapes, he only found bad fruit (Isa. 5:2). Isaiah then states that this vineyard of The Lord is the house of Israel, where God came looking for justice and righteousness, but only found bloodshed and distress (Isa. 5:7).

Back in Cardiff, Wales, I asked my long-suffering Father if he would agree to our using his garage for a few weeks and painting the windows black. My Dad eventually agreed to the inconvenience but only after reviewing our plan in great detail, but I was a little disturbed when my dad declined our offer to become an investor in our mushroom growing empire.

Mac and I then pooled our meager financial resources. We placed our order and then turned the garage into a greenhouse with hardly a chink of light coming through from outside.

After an interminable wait of at least three weeks, a large package arrived at the Dolan household. We set everything up in the trays on shelves; we followed the directions to the letter; we did well; we were established in the mushroom growing business.

In today's Gospel, Jesus contrasts himself with Israel by identifying himself as the true vine. Though Israel was a vine, it was a fruitless one and not the true vine. Jesus comes and surpasses Israel in every way, being complete as the true source of life for any person who wants to have that life. God the Father is the gardener who planted both the old Jewish Vine and the True Vine. He plants His Son in the world so that humanity may have life in him.

"Disciples must remain in the love of Jesus, the True Vine, and allow his words to remain in them in order to glorify God with a fruit-filled life."

We checked on the mushrooms every morning and every day after school. Well, we really didn't check on the mushrooms; we checked on the place where the mushrooms should have been. There wasn't one single mushroom, nothing, no fruit from our labors; nothing. After two weeks of waiting my mother was still saying, "Be patient, John, it's much too soon." Always hopeful, always supportive, always loving - thanks, Mum.

For us Christians to remain in Christ is to remain in his love. To remain in his love is to be nurtured by his love, but it is also to obey his instructions, to be obedient to him. Jesus sets the perfect example of remaining in the Father's love in obedience to Him, so Jesus exhorts us as his disciples to do the same. Love and obedience go hand in hand. Love compels one to be in union with Christ and to obey his commands. Though he would soon face death on the cross, Jesus' joy is being at one with God and doing His will. Though the disciples would soon lose their Lord Jesus on earth, they can have this true joy if they remain in his love. Jesus commands them to have mutual love for each other just as he has loved them.

There was no lack of attention to our mushroom growing. We even tossed out some of the trays, trying to prune our vine to put more spores in a smaller area. Nothing worked; the mushrooms would simply not appear. We were so disappointed. Reluctantly we made the hard decision: we would abandon the venture. And once again having my dad's permission, we would pile all the fertilized soil, spores and all, on my dad's compost heap at the "bottom of the garden" or in American English "at the back of the yard". Failure; I can still taste it. But again my mum's words, "This has been great learning experience, John; you will use this later in life." Little did Mum know how true were her words.

God is the gardener who prunes the fruitful branches so that they can bear more fruit. As we abide in Christ and bear fruit, we must acknowledge that God's pruning in our lives is to make us even more fruitful. He will cleanse us of anything that may hinder us from becoming more Christ-like in character. Sometimes the pruning can be a difficult and painful process. It can involve school, job, relationships, marriage, children, death, letting go, moving on, and anything else that we face in life. We all encounter trials as we go through this life in this world. However, when we abide in Christ, God will use these trials to shape us more into the character of His Son. This allows us to bear even more fruit for God's glory.

It was just a couple of days after we had dumped our precious would-be mushroom investment on my dad's compost heap. My mum was hanging out the washing to dry. "John," she shouted, "you had better come here right now." The ever-obedient son ran to his Mother's side; and there growing on the compost heap was a single mushroom, but not any ordinary, everyday kind of mushroom: this was one huge mushroom the size of a dinner plate.

That evening we had an inquest: why did the mushroom grow on the compost heap but not in the garage? What was different? My dad confirmed with me, "You did follow the directions?" I answered, "Of course!" My dad went on, " ...and you planted the correct number of spores?" "Yes, I followed the directions, and mixed the right consistency of fertilizer." I answered "Yes, dad, I was very careful." Then my dad went on, " ... and watered them regularly?" " Water?" I said. "That wasn't in the instructions!"

Jesus, through our baptism chooses us to bear fruit in our lives as Christians. It is not an optional thing for us to bear fruit; and we can only bear fruit through nurturing each other not just with the water of baptism but with the power of the love of Jesus.

Without the nurturing power of love and without following God's instructions, we will end up like the mushrooms starved of the nurturing life giving power of water. We can have all the best intentions in the world, but without love we will bear no fruit. We will simply break off and die like a dead branch. We must bear fruit because Jesus has chosen and appointed us to do so. That is why he stresses abiding in him; it is the only way we can bear fruit. This will bring glory to God; it will show that we are his true disciples, and it will bring joy and fulfillment to our lives both on earth and in heaven.

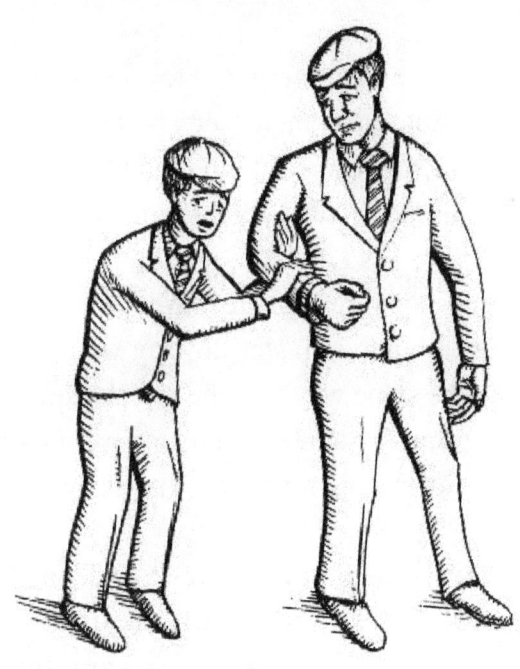

The power arising from humility

Peter said to him, "You will never wash my feet." Jesus answered, "Unless I wash you, you have no share with me."

I would like to reflect for a few moments on our journey together through Holy Week, this, the Church's most Holy time. The week is a long, at times difficult, journey. It is a week filled with intense, contrasting human emotions. There is the joy at the triumphal entry of Jesus into Jerusalem last Sunday, the escalating tensions between Jesus and the Jewish religious hierarchy. In the Gospel last night we heard the wonder at the revealing by Jesus to his disciples of the meaning of true and absolute love, agape, the love of God.

There is the love, intimacy and humility of tonight's foot washing, and then there is the apprehension, the fear of what was ahead, the pain and suffering of the Cross and then, the joy and celebration of the Resurrected Christ.

The experience of Holy Week has been likened to standing under an ever faster flowing waterfall of experiences, but in the same way that the sun shining on a waterfall creates a rainbow, so Jesus creates a rainbow in our emotional waterfall, the rainbow of promise in the resurrection.

This is the first Holy week since my Ordination as a deacon, and it is as if I feel the intensity of feelings on the journey through this week more than ever before. But there is another feeling, the feeling of the closeness of Jesus, of our being loved and cared for every step of the way; even in the darkest hour Jesus is with us. Jesus loves us and shows us how we must love each other. This is why we are here tonight; this is truly what it is all about.

This closeness to Jesus is demonstrated in the foot washing as described in John's Gospel. Peter did not feel it appropriate that his Lord and Master should wash his feet. Foot washing was the most menial of tasks, assigned to the most junior slave. Jesus used the act of foot washing to break down barriers, the class structure of master and servant, to break through cultural barriers, to get to the very root of the meaning of Christian love. *"Unless I wash you, you have no share of me."*

When I was fifteen years old I attended Cardiff High School for Boys in South Wales. The school was about a forty minute journey from our family home, a trip that involved two short walks, a bus trip to downtown Cardiff, a change of buses and another bus to the vicinity of our school. On a good day the trip was a breeze, and it was often great fun. There were no school buses in Wales in those days, so we were on public buses, with kids from other schools, including girls I might add. We were all mixed up with people going to work, there was potential for a lot of fun on those buses, and I assure you that potential was frequently realized!

For me at that time in my life, that journey to school could sometimes be quite a different experience. It could be plain torture. As a child and adolescent, I suffered for many years with severe asthma. On occasions, as I sat on the bus, the thought of the struggle ahead, just getting off the bus and walking fifty yards to school was almost unbearable.

But the pain was not just physical. I was ashamed to be seen in public like this. I would isolate myself on the bus. I would not talk to anyone. I didn't want even my closest friends to see the normally strong, athletic John as an ashen- faced bent over, wheezing cripple.

John saw himself as a leader in school, a school Monitor; he was in the academic advanced stream, a guy that always appeared in control of things. How could he be seen in such a weak, pathetic state as this?

One morning I will never forget: I had experienced an asthma attack after leaving home. I was feeling desperate, at the point of getting ready to get off the bus and return home. Then I felt a hand on my arm: "John, I have got you. Just lean on me, no one will notice, you will be OK, and we will be in school in no time." I looked up and it was my friend "Mac". Mac was known to many as the friendly giant. At sixteen he was already 6 feet 6 inches and two hundred pounds. Because Mac was about to leave school to go into the Royal Air Force, we didn't mix much anymore in the absurdly hierarchical world that was Cardiff High School.

I got out of my seat on the bus, leaned heavily on Mac's arm, and soon I was safe in school at my desk. Mac showed his love for me that day. He washed my feet; and by overcoming my pride and allowing him to help me, I also washed Mac's feet that day on that Cardiff bus.

Jesus, by the foot washing in the upper room was showing Peter and the rest of his disciples that a new authority lies in humility and being a good servant to others, rather than authority from title or position or earthly power.

In just a few moments, as we wash each other's feet tonight, please think about Mac the gentle giant so many years ago, and how he was doing exactly what Jesus was teaching us in the Upper Room. Let us reflect also on our own encounters with our own Macs in our lives and how the experiences teach us to wash each others' feet, to love and care for each other in the same way that Jesus loves us and cares for us, and is with us tonight and for always.

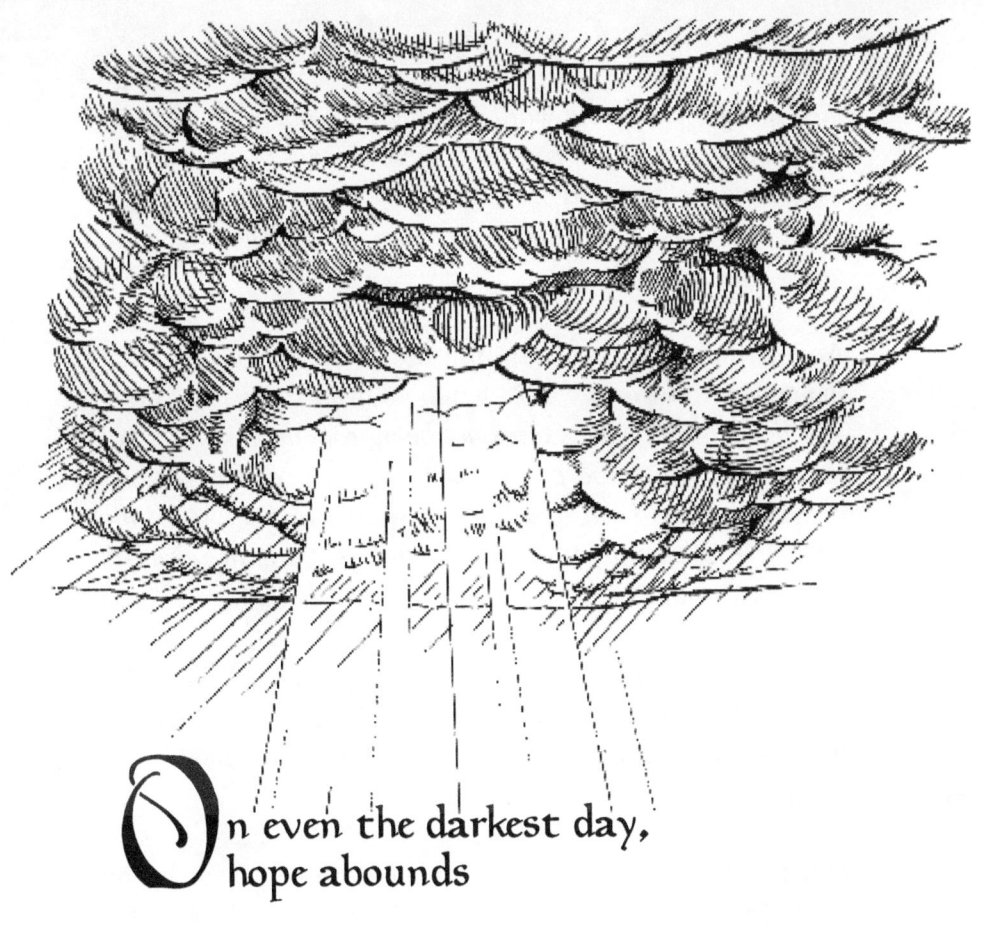

On even the darkest day, hope abounds

As we gather on this day we are within two weeks of the end of the Church year, and the readings today are all about the ending of the world. At first glance the readings are about as gray and gloomy as the skies over La Grange, Illinois these past few weeks.

Fierce winds and rain seem a suitable backdrop to today's readings. The end of the world is at hand... Daniel's visions of the Archangel Michael coming to rescue the faithful Jews from the fires of consummation... *"There shall be a time of anguish such as has never occurred since nations first came into existence. But at that time your people shall be delivered, everyone who is found written in the book."*

In Paul's letter to the Hebrews, *"For yet in a very little while,*

61

the one who is coming will come and will not delay; but my righteous one will live by faith. My soul takes no pleasure in anyone who shrinks back... But we are not among those who shrink back and so are lost... but among those who have faith and so are saved."

And in Mark's Gospel Jesus himself appeared to believe that the end of the world was at hand: *"For in those days there will be suffering such as has not been from the beginning of the creation that God created until now, no, and never will be... And if the Lord had not cut short those days no one would be saved, but for the sake of the elect, whom he chose, he has cut short those days."*

Well, if you think the skies were gray and gloomy over La Grange this past week, you should have experienced a beach holiday in August on the south coast of England in the 1950s.

Our family would visit my grandmother every year in the second week in August. We would travel to the small seaside town called Gosport near the city of Portsmouth. It was quite usual for it to rain six days out of the seven we were there. I remember looking out of the back window of my grandmother's house at the dull slate-gray sky, the wind howling through the Second World War bomb shelter still sitting in the back yard. The rain, driven sideways by the wind, would sheet on the windowpane making the view look rather like a waterfall. It was depressing to say the least. This was our only vacation time all year and it felt like the end of the world was at hand, one way or another, because the worries of the day were not limited to the inclement weather; there were also the atom bomb tests in the South Pacific.

My grandmother had a skill in linking all the gloomy news together. She would say that the bad weather was entirely due to those Russian H-bomb tests. It was interesting she never blamed the American or British tests; it was always those Russians.

But there was another side to my grandmother. She would tell me every day to look at the sky and see if I could see enough blue sky to make a patch on a Dutchman's pants. If there was, then she would predict that the sun would come out later, and we could all go down to the beach.

And do you know... some days it worked. My grandmother then proceeded to take all the credit for the improved weather, but she never made any comment if it kept on raining!

But what my grandmother did do was provide us hope every day. On even the darkest day, hope abounded in that little house. Hope that at least we could have a paddle in the ocean. Hope that the day would turn out just fine for us.

I might add that the ocean water often proved so cold it took our breath away.

In all of today's readings there are predictions of the apocalypse, the expectation of an imminent cosmic cataclysm in which God destroys the ruling powers of evil and raises the righteous to life in a messianic kingdom.

In my lifetime there have been numerous events that have led us to consider the possibility of life on this planet coming to an end. The Nazi threat, the threat of Nuclear winter (remember the drills in school to protect us from the A- bomb blast?), the growing gap in the ozone layer causing the ice caps to melt and flood our cities. The odds of huge meteorites striking the earth, the ongoing fight against global terrorism, AIDS and other incurable diseases.

But with all the dangers there is always hope; and so it is with today's scripture, there is hope for the righteous. As Christians, our hope is in the Risen Lord Jesus. Our hope arising from our faith in our Lord Jesus is stronger than the hardest granite and more predictable than the sun rising tomorrow morning.

Vaclav Havel says, "Hope is a state of mind, not of the world. Hope, in this deep and powerful sense, is not the same as joy that things are going well, or willingness to invest in enterprises that are obviously heading for success, but rather an ability to work for something because it is good."

Jesus, and the author of Hebrews, encourage us to endure for the sake of the kingdom. When we are in our darkest moments, when we are trapped with no positive end in sight, what we can do is hope on our Lord, that God will use our fear and our suffering and turn it to good.

To hope that Jesus will reveal to us the small patch of blue sky that will transform the world from a gray, dark, cold, rain swept place into a world of sunshine and light…and of life everlasting in the Kingdom of God.

Fellow Christians, let us work and work hard to find the blue sky. Let us be courageous and strong… and let us invest our time and our resources to build Christ's community of faith.

Let us turn to hope in the Light of the World, the hope of our redemption, and the promise of God's Kingdom.

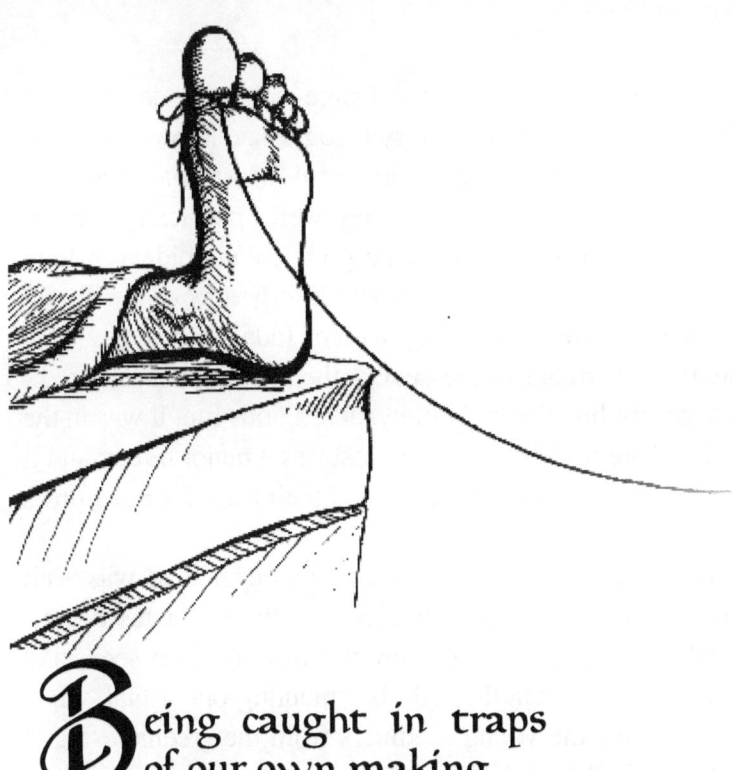

Being caught in traps of our own making

"Then the Pharisees went and plotted to trap him in what he said"…

Once again the Pharisees are waiting for Jesus to make a mistake, the inevitable slip up that will allow them to pounce on him and destroy him. They spin their elaborate webs to catch our Lord, but once again in today's Gospel we hear how Jesus outsmarts them and the Pharisees get trapped in their own trap.

In scripture we frequently hear about "The Pharisees". Who were they and why were they hounding Jesus? The name Pharisee is probably derived from the Hebrew 'perushim' or the Aramaic "perishaya", both meaning "the separated ones". It is unclear from whom exactly they were separated, but they were a distinct sect in Jewish society.

The Pharisees were neither a fringe nor extreme element; rather they were rooted in the synagogue and known for pious living, tithing, and for being prayerful. Most Pharisees were lay people rather than priests; they were 'politically correct' and they were respected as being principal upholders of Jewish traditions and moral values and interpreters of the Torah. The Pharisees were at the very heart of Judaism, but they were more the "guardians of the details, the ancient rites and traditions, not the big picture" in Jewish religious life. It was in the details where the Pharisees saw Jesus as a major threat; and it was in the details that they designed their traps for our Lord.

My dad, Walter Dolan, was a fine gardener, and was well known in our community in Llandaff, Wales for his beautiful dahlias and roses. He grew the flowers from seed, and every spring we went through the "planting-out" ritual, when he would take the young seedlings from the greenhouse and plant them in the yards front and back.

One year he had some particularly promising seedlings to plant and spent most of one Saturday carefully arranging them in a flowerbed in our front yard.

The following morning my dad discovered a thief had come in the night and had stolen all his plants; he or she had actually dug them up out of our garden. When my dad's anger had subsided he decided to replace the flowers and to lay a trap for the thief. The following weekend he planted the flowers as before. This time, however, my dad planned to attach a length of fishing line one end to the plant, the other end to run across the lawn, up the wall, through the bedroom window and to be tied to his big toe in bed. The plan was that if the thief returned, then as the plant was being stolen, the fishing line would jerk dad's big toe. This would awaken my dad and he would be able to catch the thief. My mother thought my dad was crazy and she let him know it in no uncertain terms...that he was obsessing about the plants and was endangering us all in some way with his hair-brain scheme. Nothing, however, would deter my dad from his plan to trap the thief.

Despite my mom's concerns the trap was laid.

In the middle of the night the thief struck again, but the plan went awry; the fishing line dislocated my dad's big toe, and we ended up first at the emergency room, and then at the police station. My Mom was right: my Dad got caught in his own trap. He was so obsessed with the details of his plan that he lost sight of the big picture… and suffered for it. He also heard about it for years to come!

The Pharisees were so busy with the details of their plan to squash this irritant that persisted in changing things the way they always had been. This threat to their role of guardian of religious rites, this outspoken revolutionary, this Jesus the Galilean… that they totally missed the big picture. Jesus is indeed the Messiah, the son of David, who has brought us the greatest news of all time, the Good News of life everlasting in the arms of a God, that loves each one of us, totally and unconditionally.

We all, at times get caught in traps of our own making. We are so busy being concerned about immediate issues, or perceived threats, that we lose sight of what is really important.

I see this going on in our home village right now, a community we have lived in for twenty-one years. I am certain the opponents to the Homeless Shelter, "BEDS" program being housed in our community, are not evil people. They have genuine concerns for the safety of their families. But I sense underlying issues. The purchase of a new $600,000 home and the payment of $10,000 a year in property tax does not buy insulation and blinders from the needs of the less fortunate in our society. I also see a litigious society once again hiring attorneys for their respective camps, of a drawn out detailed legal process hindering our ministry to the homeless.

Let us pray that as with the Pharisees two thousand years ago, that all involved in our village and the shelter issue will look beyond the details and keep focused on the bigger picture, the needs of the homeless. Let us be reminded of the words of the Deacons Ordination service: "In the name of Jesus Christ you are to serve all people, particularly the poor, the weak, the sick and the lonely."

Let us pray for healing in our village, for the work of the homeless shelter and all other outreach ministries in our communities.

Let us pray for ourselves, for all human beings, that we not be divided by details, that we focus together on the picture of Jesus alive within us, and of the Good News he brings of a loving and caring God. A God who loves all people equally and totally… including the homeless, the Pharisees, the thief in Wales, the Community where we live, and all of us here today.

Be alert! Evil may be lurking behind any door

"Then Jesus said to him, 'What do you want me to do for you?' The blind man said to him, 'My teacher, let me see again.'"

We are told in Mark's Gospel that Bartimaeus, son of Timaeus, regained his sight because he reached out with a loud voice to Jesus Christ, his Lord and teacher. We are not told how Bartimaeus lost his sight. Perhaps from a disease, perhaps a traumatic accident. Perhaps he had been the subject of a physical attack. Whatever happened to Bartimaeus, being blind must have totally changed his life. The picture we are given is that his loss of eyesight had reduced him to a state of dire poverty, a blind beggar sitting by the roadside eking out a living based on the occasional person's generosity and compassion.

Bartimaeus was cured by Jesus of his blindness, but the

healing is only the beginning of the story. The new eyesight undoubtedly provided Bartemaeus with a dramatic new vision of the world. With his eyesight restored by Jesus came a world of hope, a world filled with the abundance of God's love. A world where one is never alone because of the living presence of our Lord Jesus. It is a world very different from the filth and degradation of the gutters of the streets of Jericho, the total loneliness when one is blind to the reality of Jesus Christ.

The lack of vision experienced by Bartimaeus reminds me of the blindness experienced by whole societies, when they are manipulated or seduced by evil disguised as a political dictator or other despot. Nations and peoples through the ages have been manipulated to believe the world is something that it is not; and invariably it is a world devoid of the loving presence of Jesus Christ.

In 1961, just sixteen years after the end of the war in Europe, I was invited by a church group to spend a whole summer in a town called Westerstede in Northern Germany.

I stayed on a farm about five miles outside of the town, frequently bicycling into town to meet up with my friend Mac who was also part of the exchange program but who was staying with the local doctor, Dr. Peter Meyer.

Life on the farm, at first, was a very different and interesting experience and it was tranquil, but other than Gerhard, the guy my age who was technically my host, there were no men around anywhere. Even the farmhands were women. I was soon to realize what should have been obvious to me: that all the male members of the family had died in the war.

One morning, Gerhard's grandmother, very much the stern matriarch of the farming community, raised the subject of the war. As if from out of nowhere she conveyed to me in no uncertain words that the Post family played no part in the war.

"We always knew that Hitler was evil... it was the actions of a vocal minority that voted him in, and caused all the problems. The Post family would never have agreed with the terrible things that happened in Nazi Germany." Grandma Post continued, "During the war the local authorities kept all citizens in the dark. They were unaware of any wrongdoing; it was not their fault that such terrible things happened." I liked Gerhard's grandma and I believed every word she said. How could they, simple farming folk in a remote part of Germany, have changed anything? They could not have had any knowledge, any sight of the reality of what was going on...

The Gospel image today is of the blind beggar Bartamaeus sitting by the side of the road. Bartamaeus was physically blind, but he was fully aware of the reality that was going on, that Jesus the healer was there in Jericho. In modern times our streets also contain beggars, men and women driven to poverty frequently by addiction and mental illness. Lonely people, who are not fully aware of reality, people who are often blind to the loving presence of our Lord Jesus Christ.

In Germany, during that long, long, summer, my relationship with Gerhard and his family was wearing thin, particularly with Grandma Post. There was something about my situation there that made me increasingly uncomfortable. Framed photos of deceased relatives in German uniforms that I had noticed when I first arrived were no longer on display. There were furtive whispers to each other, particularly between Grandma Post and the farmhands. Guilty looks when I entered the room.

But there was one exception: Gerhard's mother Christina,

who was the church member in Westerstede, who had arranged the visit, was kind and generous to me, simply a delightful person to be with. I remember her for her kindness to me. Christina made me very welcome.

Then one evening I was in the basement of the house looking for Gerhard, and there, hanging on a hook behind a storeroom door, was a Nazi officer's uniform; as if straight out of a movie, with the SS insignia right there on the lapels. The framed photographs, that had previously been on display in the house when I first arrived were piled on a table; and looking at them I saw one of them was of Gerhard's grandfather wearing the same SS uniform hanging there on the door. As a seventeen year old, with the Second World War a very recent memory, this was a frightening experience.

Ten minutes later, with my suitcase balanced on the handlebars, I was out of there. I headed as fast as I could pedal my bicycle, to Dr Meyer's house in the town.

Dr. Meyer sat down with my friend Mac and myself and told us the whole story. Gerhard's grandmother had been, from the very beginning, an ardent member of the Nazi party, and her husband soon became a senior, highly trusted officer in the feared Waffen SS. The occupying forces after the war, and the German community had seen him as a cruel war criminal, and he served a ten-year sentence for war crimes, finally dying in prison. Their daughter Christina, Gerhard's mother, had been in the Hitler youth and had also been very active supporting Nazi ambitions.

The blind beggar Bartimaeus knew what was going on in Jericho. He knew that Jesus was in town, and he was able to shout out and reach Jesus to be cured of his physical blindness. Many persons suffering from spiritual blindness do not know Jesus. They need help to recognize our Lord even to have the opportunity to be cured. This is an area of real challenge for us Christians. To come together, to reach out to the afflicted, and let them know about Jesus, and that He is the answer in their lives.

Unlike the blind beggar Bartmaeus, Grandma Post had become spiritually blind, blind to all the wrongdoing in the war years and disowning any responsibility for her part in the evil. No one knew if she was repentant for what had happened, but it was as if she was also a blind beggar, disconnected from the real world, just existing in the gutter of her lies, waiting to die.

Gerhard's mother Christina was so very different. Although she was seduced by the evil of Hitler's time, she then found Jesus Christ in her life. Jesus did not just heal Christina's blindness, Jesus made her his disciple. Christina was active in her church and was involved in missionary work. Her kindness to me was just the way she was, the way she lived her life.

Jesus cured Christina's blindness and led her to a new life in Christ. Grandma Post, on the other hand, was still sitting by the roadside, blind, disconnected both from reality and from our Lord Jesus.

Jesus healed both Bartemaeus and Christina from their blindness. Our Lord provided them both with a new life... full of hope... full of love and with the promise of life everlasting.

Let us pray for the soul of Grandma Post, for the thousands if not millions of beggars in modern day cities and for all of us who struggle with spiritual blindness, that we all may find and be cured by Jesus Christ our Lord and Savior.

God provides a full measure for all of us; no favoritism

From the Gospel according to St. Matthew, "Am I not allowed to do what I choose with what belongs to me? Or are you envious because I am generous?"

'Life, Liberty and the Pursuit of Happiness' are three values that were at the heart of the American War of Independence against the British more than 200 years ago, values that America and Britain now share in an Alliance in the world that appears stronger than if we were one nation. It is an alliance between two nations that appears willing to take on anyone, anywhere at anytime in the world in the pursuit of protecting our values, values that tend to be wrapped up in a single word... Freedom.

The landowner in today's gospel knew all about freedom. He was the boss… he could set the hours his employees worked. He could set the minimum wage or not. There is no mention of organized labor, no Vineyard Workers Union. Why couldn't the Landowner do what he chose with what was his? It was a free world after all wasn't it… in Roman occupied, Jewish Sanhedrin dominated Israel at the time of our Lord's teachings.

We all understand very clearly that personal Freedom, even in a modern day democratic society, has some caveats attached. Freedom means freedom within the law, and from the words of my own lawyer, the law in large part is based on our heritage. Not only our heritage from England and other places in recent times but a heritage dating back to the time of Abraham.

Our Freedom is based on certain fundamental principles that have flowed down through the centuries. Principles such as reasonableness and fairness.

The laborers in the vineyard who had worked the whole day long, under the hot sun, I am sure were not amused when they received the same wage as those laborers hired at 5 o'clock in the afternoon. This was unfair, and should not be tolerated. The Landowner acted unfairly to the day laborers and in modern society he would be a target for a lawsuit. The Landowner's plea *"Am I not allowed to do what I choose with what belongs to me?"* This would hardly hold up in a world of fair labor practices. And *"are we jealous of his being generous?"* I can hear the Judge's statement now: "Generosity is quite irrelevant to the issue, there are standards of reasonableness and fairness laid down."

Fairness... being treated fairly in this life is a very important issue to most of us in our lives. Being treated unfairly attacks our very persona. We feel hurt and we feel angry...

When growing up in Cardiff, Wales, Cardiff High School for Boys was considered nationally in Britain as one of the top academic High Schools of its day. The measure used to give this rating was the number of 'State Scholarships' granted to boys from the school. This usually meant the number of boys that gained admission to Oxford or Cambridge Universities, the equivalent of four year scholarships to Harvard, Princeton or Yale.

I was taking a mathematics calculus class and I was flunking. So I approached the teacher for some after school help. I received no help. In fact, I was told that his job was to teach me in class and my job was to learn it. So much for that!

About a week later, I had left something in my desk, and had to return to the class after regular hours to retrieve it. One of my fellow students was sitting in the front row receiving extra tuition from the same teacher who had denied help to me. The student was his son, a good guy, and a good friend of mine.

The following day I confronted the teacher. He said to me "John, you are a nice young man, but you are not State Scholarship material. The extra tutoring you witnessed yesterday is only for a student who I consider to be a State Scholarship candidate. The reputation of the school and the future of the student deserves my extra attention". Not even an apology.

For many, fairness is the highest ethical stance. That is evidenced by the number of litigations in our society prompted by the perception of being treated unfairly. And then today we hear this parable of the unfair landowner. Is Jesus telling us that God is unfair?

No, he is not saying that God is unfair. Jesus is telling us that with the love of God, fairness and unfairness are totally irrelevant…

God not only provides a full measure for all of us, the measure is overflowing. God is lavish to an extreme for all of us. Unfairness doesn't even come into it. God removes all the ingredients that would cause unfairness. God provides all the extra tuition we would ever need, not to a select few on the good side of the tracks, but to the whole of humanity. God is lavish in his love for us all. His generosity abounds, and He expects us to love Him and each other to the same degree.

As we begin to understand the implications of this gospel it is like being slapped awake. As John Dominic Crossan describes it; we are confronted by its revelation and its insight. We are face to face with God's Kingdom with a new understanding of ourselves. One commentary described it as rather than explaining the parable, the parable explains us. We are invited to choose a new understanding: freedom with abundance, in the arms of a Living God.

Lord God, we are not envious of your being generous, rather we strive in our lives to understand the extent of your love for us. Help us to be similarly generous to ourselves and to our neighbours.

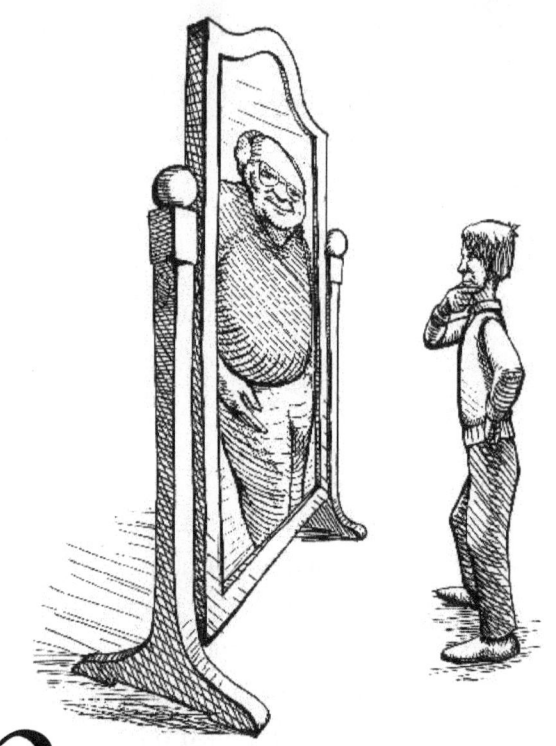

A sense of urgency to invest our talents to do God's work

"After a long time the master of those slaves came and settled accounts with his slaves... Then the one slave who had received the one talent came forward saying, 'I was afraid and hid your talent in the ground.'"

A host of good words have been written and spoken this year regarding stewardship, and our gratitude to God for all that he has given us. I cannot believe there is anyone in this community today who is unaware of the vital importance of all our pledges to the work of the church. That our pledge represents so much more than simply contributing to the Church Budget. Our pledge is a reflection of our relationship with God... every one of us... so please always be generous.

Today's readings are all about time, talents and consequences. We are reminded particularly of the fleeting nature of time and the consequences if we do not use our God-given time wisely.

Zephaniah, in our Old Testament reading, conveys warnings... warnings of the consequences if we move away from the light of a loving, caring Lord. For Zephaniah the day of the Lord was fast approaching and we must put our house in order for that coming. *"The great day of the Lord is near; near and hastening fast."*

St. Paul, writing to the Church in Thessalonica, also believes that the second coming of God is imminent and so he writes with a sense of urgency, similar to Zephaniah... but with Paul there is a major difference. The consequences of the coming of God will not be wrath and retribution; rather, the coming will be an event filled with promise. *"For God has destined us not for wrath but for obtaining salvation through our Lord Jesus Christ."*

Now we come to Matthew's Gospel and the familiar parable of the talents. Many consider this one of the more difficult parables to understand. Some people interpret the story that our Lord Jesus is a firm supporter of the Capitalist System, and I am certain the tabloid newspapers of the day could have had a field day with the story. I can just see the headlines:

"Radical Teacher Jesus proved to be a Capitalist"... "Invest in Jerusalem Bank Jesus CDs... high interest rates"... "Rabbi Jesus approves high yield investments."

With no pun intended, at face value this is how this parable reads. But of course Jesus is saying something quite different.

But before we go any further, there is a fact in today's Gospel that I am told needs some explanation. What was the nature of a "talent" in the parable? It is thought that a talent, when measuring its weight in gold, equaled what a laborer would earn in the span of 15 years in the first century, a huge amount for the severely underpaid people of those days. The word "talent" has had such a significance that, as we know, it has passed down, and is used in modern day language now as meaning a personal skill or gift.

Jesus is saying that the various and sundry talents and skills that we possess have all been given by our father in Heaven… and in the short time we have in this life we must use our talents to the benefit of God's Kingdom.

Jesus is telling us to be conscious that time slips away from us very quickly, and we must invest our talents in activities that support God's plan for this world.

Some of you may remember my stories of my dad's mom, Nana, a formidable but wise woman who lived to ninety-six years of age. Nana lived in a very small house, probably smaller than the square footage of our basement in Western Springs. Her backyard was about the size of a postage stamp, but it did have room for the world's most comfortable deck chair.

On the very occasional sunny day, as a young boy I would lie back in Nana's deck chair looking up at the white puffy clouds scudding along. I remember that time as being so quiet, so peaceful; the only sound was those of a nearby aspen tree's leaves rustling in the breeze. As an eight year old I thought life would last for ever…no responsibilities…no chores to do, I remember musing… what a joy life will be.

Jesus is telling us there are consequences if we don't keep God at the center of our lives and act accordingly. In the parable he describes the abusive behavior of the master to the slave, who he felt did not make the optimum use of his talents in the time that the master was gone.

In our lives there are consequences for letting time slip away without using our talents to further Christ's ministry in the world. The consequences are falling prey to the powers of evil, and losing the wonderful opportunity that Christ has given us of life everlasting. If we hold back rather than offer our gifts freely, we are often left with a feeling of emptiness, the same feeling we might have when a job is half completed. A sense of lack of worth. But when we display ourselves as children of Light, as Christ's own for ever, the world takes on a different look. When we feel a sense of urgency, and that there is only a limited amount of time available to us in this life, and when we then reach out and help the poor and needy, we feel different about ourselves. That is what Jesus is talking about in today's Gospel message.

One summer's day, I was having a wonderful nap in

Nana's comfortable deckchair, but suddenly I was startled by an unfamiliar voice. "What's a strong lad like you wasting your time lying around the place? There's work to be done round here! There are many people who need you, John. You don't have time to loll around in that deckchair."

The voice was that of my uncle Vernon, a thirty year officer in the Royal Navy. He had just arrived home on leave, and this was my first introduction to my lifelong friend and confidante, my uncle Vernon. My dad's younger brother is now ninety-three years old. Uncle Vernon lives in our village in Wales. I talk with him at least once a week, and uncle Vernon understands what it means to rise from humble surroundings and minimum education, to maximize his God given talents and help others in this life. Uncle Vernon has helped me so much in this life.

Forty years ago the Beatles had a hit song, "When I'm sixty- four". Being of the same generation as the Beatles, sixty-four seemed a million years away. Plenty of time to do whatever life presented me! I have learned that life goes by like the blink of an eye.

Our Lord Jesus is telling us all not to waste any more time lolling endlessly in our comfortable deck chairs. We will soon be sixty four and perhaps much more. Let us look after ourselves so that we are strong; and let us not be afraid to use our God given talents to help others. If we simply bury our talents in the ground... if we fail to optimize our God given skills, we will frequently encounter frustration and bitterness. We are left with a feeling of something missing in our lives. But when we reach out and help others, and show love and compassion. If we invest our talents in God's work, then we end up feeling fulfilled with a sense that our life has been a time of contribution to the good of others, and that we are not just old and useless but that we have made a difference for good in the world.

"When I'm sixty-four" seemed far, far away more than fifty years ago; but time indeed goes by like the blink of an eye.

In the words of the Beatles song "When I'm Sixty-Four"

When I get older, losing my hair,
Many years from now,
Will you still be sending me a Valentine
Birthday greetings, bottle of wine?

Whether we are eight years old, sixty-four or ninety-three… if we are using our God given talents in the world, we will never be lonely and never forgotten. Jesus loves us and will be with us for ever.

Risking your personal safety for your faith in Jesus Christ

From a lifetime of reading scripture, particularly reinforced from weekly Bible Study, I am convinced there is just one light, just one hope for us, in an otherwise chaotic world.

That light of course is Jesus Christ the Son of God, truly our strength and our redeemer.

There is chaos in the world as we await the birth of the Christ child in Bethlehem in just two days. We await the coming of Jesus with great anticipation, but also knowing that we live in a world where there remains great risk for being a follower of Jesus Christ.

It is easy for us living in the United States to forget the physical dangers of being a Christian, particularly in many parts of Asia Minor and East Africa. We have personally heard the stories from Archbishop Daniel of Sudan's own lips, of how his office has been repeatedly raided by the police under the orders of the radical Sudanese Islam Government. We have heard from the Bishop's wife how she has been imprisoned some ten times for her outspokenness, as head of the Anglican Mother's Union in Sudan.

There are many illustrations in Holy Scripture of persons accepting personal risk in the name of their faith.

Let us consider the context of today's reading from the Book of Isaiah.

The two arch enemies of Judah, the lands of Aram and Ephraim, had created an alliance to jointly attack and occupy Jerusalem. Aram was roughly equivalent to modern day Syria, while Ephraim was a kingdom in the northern part of modern day Israel. This alliance spelled potential disaster for Judah.

In the meantime, God had instructed Isaiah to warn Ahaz, King of Judah, of the impending attack. Obedient Isaiah puts aside any personal risk to himself (we know what frequently happens to messengers bringing bad news to Kings) and he warns King Ahaz.

Then, in today's reading, God not only reinforces Isaiah's warning about the invasion, but follows what many Christian scholars discern as a direct foretelling of the coming of Christ: "Look, the young woman is with child and shall bear a son, and shall name him Immanuel."

As we eagerly await the birth of the Baby Jesus, let us reflect on the courage we need to hold to be faithful Christians. The courage to deal with distractions from our principal ministry that our Lord vests in us, to love and care for each other.

No matter who the fellow human being is, no matter where they are from, whether they be strangers, whether they engender fear or suspicion in our minds. No matter if the persons awake prejudices that we may not even be fully conscious of. Whoever the person is, our Lord Jesus commands us to bid them welcome, and for us to love and care for them.

It is my experience that persons who suffer from depression frequently withdraw from families and society, particularly at the time of holidays. My own father at Christmas time would frequently retire to his bed with mysterious bad colds, that appeared as if out of nowhere.

In recent years I have discovered that my dad suffered with severe depression his whole life. Only one person knew of it. My Uncle Vernon, his younger brother now 94 years old, knew it from when he was a small child. My dad told him and swore him to secrecy. In recent years, some 30 years after my dad's death, my buddy, my Uncle Vernon shared with me this long-held secret about my dad. My dad was scared and ashamed of the condition. If only I had known so that I could convey even more love to him to help him through those difficult times!

Persons that suffer from depression, abuse, addictions or other afflictions in their lives, need our Christian love more than ever, as we approach the birth of Christ, the light coming into the world.

Then there are those who suffer under political regimes that are hostile to Christianity. We are told that we must love our oppressors, even those who torture us, because of our faith in the Lord Jesus. We must be brave and strong in this chaotic world, a world full of distractions, a world that is nothing without the light of the world, our Lord Jesus Christ. Jesus the one we wait for... the one who makes all the difference.

I would like to tell you a story, of one of my first-ever encounters with anti Christian influence in the world, and of a young man's willingness to accept risk as a faithful follower of our Lord.

In August of 1962 (with hindsight... just three months before the Cuban missile crisis) I had the great privilege of representing Welsh youth on a six-week government sponsored trip to the Soviet Union. Twenty-five of us were passengers on a Russian boat headed east down the Baltic Sea heading for Leningrad (now with its original name of St. Petersburg). A group of us were standing at the front (the sharp end... all right, for a certain Navy Captain in our community's benefit, the bow of the ship.)

There was a cloudless sky, and the sun was suddenly reflecting, from what, at a distance, looked like a golden mirror, and then a series of mirrors of different shapes. The sun was shining on the gold, silver and multicolored onion-shaped domes of the Cathedrals of Leningrad.

It was a sight I will never forget; and I was filled with a feeling that with beauty of this kind, the stories of repression and religious intolerance had to be figments of the Western Media, and in fact the place we were visiting may be very different from what we were led to believe.

I was soon to learn how wrong I was. Fast forward some five hours, and we were aboard a train heading for Moscow. Note that before we left the UK we had been briefed about customs and behavior. High on the list was not to bring any foreign currency or Bibles into Russia.

There were eight or ten of our group sharing a compartment on the train. If any of you have seen the movie "Dr. Zhivago" you will know exactly what the train was like. Suddenly there was a rap on the compartment door, and two armed Russian soldiers instructed us to open all our suitcases.

The soldiers searched each case in a highly aggressive and confrontational manner; and then in one of my companions' suitcase they found three Bibles. The soldiers screamed at my friend in Russian, and brought their rifles down smack on the Bibles, which were severely damaged in the onslaught. They then confiscated the Bibles. My recollection is they then said in English something like, "If you weren't accompanied by an official guide we would shoot you on the spot."

My family tell me that on occasion I tend toward exaggeration; not so with this story. I remember the feeling: we were all shaking like a leaf. But then the friend who had the Bibles quietly prayed aloud, "Oh Lord Jesus, help me to love your oppressors. I know you will never leave my side dear Jesus, and I will love and trust you for all time."

That day I learned a little of what it's like when we take a risk in the world to follow our Lord.

As we approach the birth of our beloved Christ, let us remember that we are called to risk ourselves in His name. That we must love, and care for all our fellow human beings... for radical extremists, the homeless, the depressed, the addicted, the sick and suffering, the bereaved, the military representatives of oppressive regimes... for all of God's people.

Let us remember the courage it took to take those Bibles into the Soviet Union, and the love of Christ that protected us in the face of aggression.

Let us remember to accept personal risk if it is necessary to reach out and show love and caring for our fellow human beings.

Let us pray for all of us who struggle with distractions in this busy and chaotic world, distractions that make it more difficult for us to have a full and loving relationship with God through our Lord Jesus Christ.

Wait and trust in the Lord

Many consider Isaiah to have been the greatest exhorter and encourager of the exiled people of Israel. Today's reading from the book of Isaiah reminds us down the ages that God is a lot bigger, and certainly a lot more instrumental in our lives, than we proud humans care to think.

We proud, greedy humans build great political empires, we surround ourselves with what we perceive as financial security... and in an instant it can shrink and even disappear.

When I was growing up, the immensity and power of the Soviet Union seemed a formidable foe, that would last forever; but in the space of just a few years, it crumbled, collapsed and disappeared into history.

From the Book of Isaiah: *"But those who wait for the Lord shall renew their strength, they shall mount up with wings like eagles, they shall run and not be weary, they shall walk and not faint."*

Today, the fifth Sunday after Epiphany is also known as Septuagesima Sunday. There are some approximations to be found, particularly in the ancient Church calendars, but the meaning of Septuagesima Sunday is said to be that there are seventy days left until the crucifixion of our Lord. For the mathematicians among us there are in fact only 60 days from now until Good Friday, but I already indicated we are dealing with historical approximations.

The significance of 70 days? It was customary for some Christians, usually clergy, to begin their fasting at this point. I would like you to please note that at least one member of the Emmanuel clergy, the one standing in the pulpit today, does not subscribe to this particular discipline.

Today's reading from Isaiah is described so succinctly in a recent homily by the Rev. Angela Askew: "In a magnificent reinterpretation of the first chapter of Genesis, our reading from Isaiah slowly and deliberately shows that in calling into existence the whole cosmos, God has also called into existence all the peoples of the earth. They are consequently under his divine jurisdiction as are the sun, the moon, the stars, and everything else 'on high.' Therefore, although God's understanding of the various nations and peoples may be quite inscrutable, the reach and scope of God's activities are universal and endless."

In the summer of 1962, I was privileged to be selected to represent the youth of Wales in a six week British-government sponsored, youth exchange visit to the Soviet Union. Prior to leaving the UK, the British Government gave us some rudimentary Russian lessons, including commonly used phrases. I will never forget one of those phrases, in "pidgin" Russian: "Gidea Bassin Moskva." In English, "Where is the Moscow swimming pool?" One of the great sights to see in Moscow was apparently the world's largest swimming pool, a circular pool with a diameter of some 200 yards.

Isaiah knows that even in a hostile political environment, that the Jews found themselves in, even in the harshest times of financial deprivation, God is hard at work and God is not just for the Jews but for the whole world.

Isaiah's listeners are told to wait for the Lord, but I believe waiting means trusting, even when things look hopeless.

A great moment in Russian history was the defeat of Napoleon in 1812. To celebrate the victory, the people of Moscow built, what they intended to be, the largest cathedral in the world, the Cathedral of Christ the Savior. By 1831 a huge cathedral was built with five golden domes. The Cathedral of Christ the Savior was said to be one of the most beautiful buildings in all of Russia.

In 1933, on Stalin's instructions, the Communists destroyed the Cathedral, removing every last piece of marble and leaving a large circular hole in the ground where the Cathedral once stood.

The scope of the power of God is seen in today's Gospel. Nobody and no one are outside the reach and scope of our loving God. In Mark's Gospel, demons were cast aside and were not even allowed to speak, "because they knew him". The demons recognized the total power vested in our lord Jesus by His loving Father in Heaven. The demons crumbled and collapsed in the face of our Lord.

The Communists intended that the huge round hole in the ground, that had been the foundation of the Cathedral of Christ the Savior, was to be the foundation for a massive tower building, "The Palace of the Soviets". But it was never built. Instead the hole in the ground was turned into the Bassin Moskva, the world's largest swimming pool.

Mark's Gospel today describes Jesus' work in actively building God's Kingdom in the world. Our Lord is replacing old, mistaken ideals and sickness with the Good News of God's eternal love and redemption. He is replacing old edifices and nonsense situations with new hope and love, and caring for each other. We experience a recognition of a loving God who has always been with us, but on occasion in our own pride and zealousness, we forget his presence.

In August 1962, I swam in that huge swimming pool in Moscow, so I know that it was real, or should I say surreal. But the faithful Russians, who waited patiently, received their reward. By the mid-1990s, in the post-Soviet era, the swimming pool had disappeared; and the Cathedral of Christ the Savior once again stands more glorious than ever.

I am certain that God has nothing against swimming; but it surely must make him smile that the Church has re-established itself from the persecution and difficult times under the Soviet regime.
Isaiah again tells us that beneath and behind any given hu-

man political situation, that our God is hard at work. The God of Israel is also the God of the Gentiles and His power and scope is universal.

So, in any human crisis, where a positive outcome seems impossible, we are taught to wait and trust in the Lord.

When we seem to be surrounded by bad financial news and villains in the like of Bernie Madoff. When our 401ks are now casually termed 201k, let us hold on, wait and trust in the Lord.

God will deliver us in the same way as he did in October 1962, the Cuban missile crisis. Just two months after I was swimming in the Bassin Moskva, my dad and I were huddled around the radio in our home in Cardiff, Wales, expecting at any moment to hear news of impending nuclear devastation.

The Cuban missile crisis was, of course, averted; and we will also be delivered from the current financial crisis because God is at hand working with us. All we have to do is listen to Him and act accordingly; and I believe we will.

Any pursuit in life calls for moderation except one's love of Jesus Christ

From St. Luke's Gospel "You cannot serve God and wealth (mammon)."

My dad's mom, my grandmother "Nana" was a very strong, forceful, and wise lady. She was not someone you picked an argument with because you would always lose. Nana lived a very modest, if not Spartan life in a material sense, but a life that was rich... one might say ironclad... in her strong sense of what was right and wrong.

There were no gray areas in Nana's life, and for the 96 years of her life she ruled the Dolan family roost. If she arrived for a visit and sat down in the living room without removing her hat, watch out! Someone had slipped up and she was gunning for them. The problem was she never let on right away who the victim was.

I loved Nana, and Nana was invariably nice to me. My wife Karen witnessed on a number of occasions that John was high on her list. I admired and loved her, but I admit at times, many times, to have been intimidated by Nana. Nana was a person of few words but when she spoke, everyone better listen.

I think I have always been a good listener, and I have always been similarly blessed with an excellent memory. Both skills were particularly important when Nana was doing the talking, because one can be certain the next time that you saw her she would test you on what she had told you the last time you were together.

On one occasion Nana said to me, "John, people make their lives much too complicated. Always speak the truth. It makes life so much easier because if you lie you have to remember what you said the last time you were with this particular person. If you always tell the truth you don't have to think at all."

Nana also told me the key to a happy and fulfilling life is moderation in all things, with one great exception: you must love the Lord Jesus with every bone in your body, with every thought in your mind and with every feeling in your heart. You must put Jesus first, always above all earthly things, particularly ahead of the love of money and worldly possessions, even, she added, ahead of the love of your grandmother.

I remember Nana's saying that if I, John, were to put the love of Jesus as the number one priority in life I would find life so much more satisfying than giving too high a priority to wealth and possessions.

This of course is the essence of today's Gospel. We must put God ahead of all things in our earthly life. Nothing, not even the love of our families, can match the love we must hold for Jesus Christ.

As for Mammon, from the Greek word "mamona", meaning riches, Mammon is defined in Webster's as material wealth or possessions. The love of Mammon is nothing, zilch. It is a huge zero in comparison with the priorities laid down by Jesus, that God our Father in Heaven comes first, always, and for all time.

In Luke's Gospel today, Jesus describes the actions of a steward in discounting his master's bills, so that he, the steward, would create closer ties with the debtors. This would provide refuge for the steward at the time when he loses his job.

In my opinion, the steward used mammon as a means to create closer human relationships, that will be there long after mammon fails you.

Even though the steward would probably have been the target of a lawsuit in today's litigious society, for discounting his master's invoices, it is implied without the necessary authority, he was complimented for understanding that the relationships were more important than just collecting the debts for his master. That means, of course, that the creation of an eternal relationship with God is everything, while preoccupation with chasing a few dollars in this life means nothing.

From the days as a child with my grandmother "Nana", fast forward a few years. I was sitting on a train, undoubtedly traveling between Wales and London. I was an eighteen year old, a big shot and I smoked a meerschaum pipe, so I was seated in a smoking compartment. Sitting opposite me was a young woman chain smoking cigarettes, lighting one after the other. The ash tray was full, but the pack of cigarettes was empty. She sighed, she grumbled; then she crumpled up the pack and stuffed it in the ashtray. On the cellophane wrap I could see that the brand of cigarettes was the well known English cigarette "Players Navy Cut", and written across the front of it in big letters, "They Satisfy." I said to myself, "I wonder how many cigarettes it takes to satisfy. Well, at least I know it's more than twenty in the past two hours."

I was reminded of this story by a contemporary cigarette advertisement I saw on the Internet: "Full Flavor Reds"... "the flavor of our Virginia blend appeals to the most experienced smoker. These satisfy the most." Some hopes! That is the problem with the unreasonable pursuit of worldly wealth and possessions: how much do you need to be satisfied? I also read this past week about a tobacco store in New York City. Presumably associated with the decline in cigarette sales, an opium pipe hung in the window and underneath it was a sign; "For the man who wants to forget that he has everything."

You have everything and are still not satisfied, so the only thing is to forget it some way, lose yourself in some opium dream. It is true, as our Lord said, that earthly treasures never satisfy.

Today is a day when we visibly demonstrate our love for Jesus Christ, and how much more important He is than the worship of material wealth and possessions. We love and trust Jesus Christ so much that we are willing to trust Him with those whom we hold perhaps most dear in the world, our newborn children. Two small children were baptized here in La Grange today. They have become the newest members of Christ's Community of Faith, sealed by the Holy Spirit in baptism and marked as Christ's own for ever.

Nana had it absolutely right: moderation in life in all things with the one exception, a total personal commitment to Jesus Christ. This commitment then removes any dilemma of serving two masters. Mammon is relegated to where it truly belongs.

The acquisition of earthly wealth and possessions is a God-given resource, a gift from God not intended as an end in itself but rather to make us equipped and able to pursue God's grace through the love of our Lord Jesus. Then we attain true satisfaction, happiness and fulfillment in our lives.

Stereotyping hides the loving nature of God

"Nathanael said to him, 'Can anything good come out of Nazareth?'"

It has been said that extensive study of Holy Scripture is like taking a bath in the words of human interpretation, so that after a lifetime of soaking in the waters of the Bible, one begins to have a glimpse of the real nature of God. In depth Bible study can be characterized like the appreciation of a full length movie. As for the readings we hear on Sundays and Holy Days, our adopted Lectionary is more like a series of snapshots.

But these are complex snapshots, and in themselves contain many messages from God. I believe a vital contribution to an informed Christian life is to distill these messages to the point that we are all capable of relating the message to our everyday needs. Not to bury the message in theology, however sound it may be, and not to lose the message in extensive verbiage, but rather to be clear and concise as to exactly what God is telling us.

In today's readings, we hear from the Book of Samuel that responding to God's invitation takes some of us longer than others. An important message, but for a future sermon, not for today. In contrast the message from the Psalm 63, the Psalmist is ready right away to respond to God. *"Oh God eagerly I seek you; my soul thirsts for you."* The composer of the Psalm is ready and knows that *"God's loving kindness is better than life itself"*.

Samuel waited in the Holy Temple; the Psalm's author gazed upon the Lord in the holy place. Paul tells us that through Jesus Christ we are the holy place, for our body is the temple of the Holy Spirit.

And in John's Gospel we hear that as the Lord called Samuel many years before, Jesus now invites Philip to *"follow me"*. Philip doesn't need three invitations; he jumps at the chance and he goes further by not only joining, but by recommending Jesus to his friend Nathanael.

Nathanael responds to God's message, but he has some personal obstacles to overcome before he is free to have his personal glimpse of the nature of God. One of these obstacles is Nathanael's inclination to stereotype strangers: that is if he sees someone to be different from himself and if he has heard things about "those people" then he will pull down the blinds and dismiss all people in that category.

Stereotyping people is very sad. It is sad for the person being stereotyped. But it is definitely more sad for the person doing the stereotyping, because by closing your mind in judgment against any one person in this life, you lose the opportunity to see God in the face of "those people".

Some of you have heard my stories of my dad's mom, Nana. My Nana was a strong, wonderful lady, who lived to ninety-six years. Nana was a loving grandmother who taught me a great deal about life, but Nana had iron-clad opinions about anything and everything and everybody.

When I was growing up in Britain, it was very hard to find anyone who liked the Irish. When you think back it was totally ludicrous. St. Patrick's Day was unheard of; no one had a clue what Guinness was. The hundreds of thousands of vital Irish manual workers were ridiculed. The Irish were the butt of jokes in any pub in England: Shame on me; I still remember the jokes.

The source of hatred, the jokes and stereotyping came to a climax of course in the late 1960s with the troubles in Northern Ireland, but its origin lay deep in the struggle between landed power and freedom-seeking Irish tradition. Two persons in the same boat, two races on neighboring islands, but in the pursuit of power and wealth down through the ages, the stronger abused the weaker; and in the wake of the abuse came generations of hatred and resentment, until the real issues were veiled by secondary issues such as political and religious affiliations.

Nana would have nothing to do with "those Papist Irish people" and was always very vocal about it. She would dismiss a whole nation with one sentence: "John, there is nothing good to be said about those Irish and I don't want them mentioned in this house!!" I can hear her voice now. I could never really understand why Nana was so vitriolic about her hatred of the Irish.

Nathanael's immediate reaction to the recommendation from Phillip about Jesus was based on hearsay, not about Jesus the man. This story describing Nathanael's response shows the enormous negative power of stereotyping and the huge obstacle that stereotyping can be to making good decisions in this world. Nathanel's first reaction was to dismiss Philip's compelling words, "*We have found him about whom Moses in the law and also the prophets wrote, Jesus son of Joseph from Nazareth.*" He also seemed to ignore the fact that his friend Philip had reached the conclusion to follow Jesus after personally meeting our Lord. Nathanael was more concerned about "those people" from Nazareth. Without Philip's persistence, Nathanel may have missed the greatest opportunity in his life, simply because Jesus was from Nazareth, not worth even thinking about.

Years later I discovered that my grandfather, Nana's dear, sweet husband, my granddad Poppa, my Dad's dad, was born in County Cork in Ireland. That while growing up in Wales there were only two Dolans in the White Pages; that in Dublin and Boston there were thousands of Dolans.

Nana clearly loved my granddad, Poppa, her husband Charlie. There was nothing personal about it; Nana was simply seduced by the power of stereotyping, with the end result that many of us, for many years, hated all things Irish and thus through ignorance disowned and hated part of our own heritage. Stereotyping, "the lumping of individual human lives and expressions into categories.. and then imposing judgment on those categories," is one of the world's major problems.

Whether the category be Moslems, African Americans, Gays, fat people, blue collar workers. Whether it be women drivers, Irish people, people from Nazareth or Hispanics. Whether it be Roman Catholics, Germans, people who live in Hinsdale, Jews, Indians or Polish. I believe that in making knee jerk, uninformed judgments against any category of persons, that we are the ones who suffer. We suffer because we miss the opportunity to see Christ in those persons. Through our own ignorance and obstinacy we miss the opportunity to have a glimpse of the nature of God. We are the ones who lose out, in the same way that Nathanel almost missed knowing the Christ.

All of us human beings are made in the image of God. The face of Christ can be seen in the most unlikely of persons; but our hearts must be open and unbiased so that we may receive him.

In the words of the Baptismal Covenant that we renewed in this place just last Sunday, "Will you seek and serve Christ in all persons, loving your neighbor as yourself?" And we responded, "We will with God's help."

No free lunches in this life

"Jesus said, 'And whoever does not take up the cross and follow me is not worthy of me'".

There are some tough words and difficult choices in today's Gospel. In order for us to appreciate their full meaning, let us for a moment consider the context.

Jesus is preparing his disciples for the enormous responsibility that lies ahead, when it will be up to them to spread His message throughout the world. This is the time for commissioning his disciples.

Jesus is instructing them in the ground rules, the fundamental choices that have to be made in order to be a Christian. Jesus "cuts to the chase": the choice is that we must love and put our trust in Jesus above everything else in this life, even if that means putting our very lives at risk. Only those who accept the threat of destruction will find eternal life. Whoever does not take up the cross is not worthy of me.

Many of you know Joan, my mum from Llandaff, Wales, a regular and much welcomed visitor here. I don't think any of you, other than my wife Karen and daughter Michelle, knew my dad, Walter.

I loved my dad, a strong, intelligent, wise man. A gentle man, a man who would tell Michelle stories about a mysterious Mr. Flatman who arrived in a box from the hardware store, and lived in the mailbox down the road from our home in Western Springs, IL.

My dad was a conservative man, a musician, an electrical engineer and an Anglican from birth. Dad was clerk of the vestry at Llandaff Cathedral for fifteen years, truly a living stone of that ancient Cathedral.

One of the less endearing characteristics of Dad, at least for a teenager and young John growing up fiercely independent, was that Dad would never, ever, let me avoid the tough issues. My dad invariably made good choices, which was even more irritating to a youngster who thought he knew pretty much everything there was to know about the world. But right until his death in 1981, he would not hesitate in letting me know what choices I should make, whether I wanted to hear them or not!

I recall a couple of those times when my dad presented me with difficult choices.

At 24 years of age, my involvement in the sport of rowing meant everything to me, to the expense of my British CPA license, attending Church and pretty much all other things in my life. Dad, shall we say, helped me make a tough choice, he set my priorities straight, and he did not mince his words in the process.

On another occasion, some years earlier, Dad and I agreed on a set of ground rules for the rare event of John's borrowing Dad's car for an important date. A set of rules which I, in my 18 year old wisdom, chose to totally ignore, a bad choice resulting in much trouble, the details of which hardly fit the image of the Deacon relaying this story. My ears still tingle from my dad's "helping me learn" from the bad choices I made that night.

In Matthew's Gospel, Jesus is also laying it on his disciples with no holds barred; he is in effect saying, "There are tough issues you have to face and choices you have to make if you are to find salvation in me, your Lord and Savior. Be steadfast in your love and trust in me. Put me first always, do not get disconnected from me, suffer for me and you will then be worthy of me."

I am sure we all remember certain words or phrases used by our parents. In fact at times we find ourselves using exactly the same words with our own kids, words that annoyed us so much, so many years ago. I hear myself saying my dad's words said to me: "John, you appear to be under the mistaken impression that the world somehow owes you a living." I hear Dad also saying, "Who told you that everything in life was going to be easy, what makes you any different from the rest of us?"

I also hear him saying, " You have to understand it's not the troubles and suffering in life that are important, it's how you live and cope with those problems that counts." I also hear, "All the money and possessions in the world won't make any difference; get your body over to that Church and contribute." Tough words and even tougher choices that had to be made.

Tough words, difficult choices from a dad who loved his son. I was very fortunate in having a dad who cared for me and wanted me to have a full and meaningful life.

Jesus never said our journey in this life would be easy. He was not with us to hand out tickets to Disneyworld, to provide free lunches, or to remove our pain and suffering. What Jesus did tell us was that if we made the right choices, if we love him and trust him above all things, then He is with us at every step on our journey, he is with us now and forever, to guide, strengthen, nurture, love and help us cope. He is with us to help us pick up the cross so that we are worthy of Him, and so reach our destination of life everlasting with our Father in heaven.

Jesus presented his disciples, and all of us here this morning, with these difficult choices, because like my dad and his son John, Jesus loves us unconditionally, for all time.

God's gifts are for the benefit of all God's creatures

In St. Matthew's Gospel Jesus said to the twelve apostles: "Whatever town or village you enter, find out who in it is worthy, and stay there until you leave. As you enter the house greet it. If the house is worthy, let your peace come upon it; but if it is not worthy, let your peace return to you. If anyone will not welcome you, or listen to your words, shake off the dust from your feet as you leave that house or town."

It just happens there were twelve members of our regular weekly Bible study group scheduled to meet at our house this past Wednesday. For one of the only times in the past year and a half we had to cancel, and it became necessary to contact twelve persons at the last moment. Through the wonders of modern technology, e-mail, fax, telephone, cell phone, voice-mail, and physically passing the word, by some miracle nobody showed at our door at seven o'clock expecting Bible Study.

This scheduling experience reminded me of the golden virtues of the secretaries of this world. Then I began to think about the countless gatherings and meetings that Jesus held with his twelve companions, and probably thousands of others. I wonder who organized Jesus' schedule?

I posed this question to a certain scholarly soul among us and he remarked, "I have no idea but it sure must have been a lousy and difficult job."

Today's Gospel reminds me of a military briefing before a flight sortie, or a foray into territory which is in dispute but which is vital to be reclaimed. You don't know exactly where the enemy is, but you have preselected the targets and so now you will test the waters.

The Commander in Chief of his spiritual army, Jesus Christ, was very clear in his directions to the twelve. Their primary mission was to take the Good News to the lost sheep of the house of Israel. Jesus told his disciples "Leave the Gentiles and the Samaritans, at least for the time being, and focus on our own kind. Let us visit all Jewish people in all houses in all neighborhoods, put personal preferences aside, no exceptions."

Jesus tells his twelve apostles, "Let you use every God given skill that you have, as you bring the Good News to the lost sheep of the House of Israel. Strengthen yourselves with the power of the Holy Spirit to heal the sick, lift up the faint hearted, comfort the bereaved, raise the dead, all for my name's sake."

Jesus continues, "If you meet resistance as you enter a house, shake off any resistance to your mission as if it were mere dirt on your sandals and then move right on down the road. Let us get the job done. The time available to do God's work here on earth is severely limited by our human frailty. Let us get on with it; the Kingdom of heaven is at hand."

For those in the congregation that think or hope that I have run out of stories from my childhood in Wales, I am afraid you are going to be sadly disappointed. What's more, Karen and I will be in Wales next week. No doubt even more stories will emerge after extensive Black Lion conversations with my 93 year old Uncle Vernon, my friend Nigel and many others.

A few of you may remember my late mother, Joan Dolan, a frequent visitor to Emmanuel. Joan was a particularly outgoing, friendly person. My sister Lizzie inherits those character traits.

Joan Dolan had a couple of friends in our village who were not your run of the mill, average, middle class lady types. One of these "unusual" friends was a certain Hilary Harmsworth.

Word had it that "Mrs. Harmsworth" hated kids, so for years I had kept a safe distance from Hilary Harmsworth's house. It was also said that she really didn't like any human beings, but that she loved all other kinds of God's creatures. Rumor said that she captured stray cats and dogs, wild otters, birds, squirrels; in fact she would grab any wildlife that happened to be in the vicinity of her small shuttered cottage.

The local kids, myself included, kept well away from Mrs. Harmsworth and her animal prisoners. It was said that years ago one of the kids even found a used cauldron in the woodshed at the bottom of the Harmsworth garden.

I really believed Hilary Harmsworth was evil. I even walked around the block to avoid her house. My mum asked me on a number of occasions to go with her to visit her friend, but there was no way on God's green earth that I was ever going to enter the Harmsworth house.

In today's Gospel, Jesus again focuses on the fundamentals for our lives of Christian faith and action. We are not to be waylaid by false promises nor by people who see the world in a different way. Our task as Christians is to reveal to the world the true nature of our loving, forgiving, generous God and to work hard in his name. We are required, not requested. to do His work in this world and we are told to visit all places, all villages, towns and homes, even those places where we would rather not go. We are told to visit and contribute to the physically deprived nation of the Sudan. We are told to raise money for outreach projects, to reach out and take the Good News of Jesus Christ to all who will listen, to visit people's homes, to seek out who is worthy and to unite those persons into the body of Christ's Community of Faith.

Back in our family home in Wales… one evening my mom received an urgent phone call from Hilary Harmsworth. She said she needed to be hospitalized the next day, and that she had no one to look after the animals. My dad was not available that evening, so I found myself in the position that I really had no choice but to accompany my mum and help out. A few minutes later we were entering Mrs. Harmsworth's cottage. All I remember is feeling scared to death about Mrs. Harmsworth and her reputation and what we would find inside her house.

In today's Gospel, the apostles were dispatched on their mission with no luggage or belongings, no money or any other assistance or resources. They had been told by Jesus that they had all the resources that they would ever need in the power of God's love. The apostles were on God's business, and they should use their time productively. They should be steadfast and have no fear and they should not be limited by any preconceptions or bias about the people they were to visit.

Regardless of their backgrounds and experience, regardless of what dangers or difficulties they might encounter as they enter people's houses, the apostles' job was to bring the Good News of Jesus Christ to all of God's own people…the children of Israel.

Hilary Harmsworth's house was a sight to behold. Hilary herself was dressed in a brightly colored outfit reminding me of a fortune teller, with a silk scarf around her hair. She was reclining on an overstuffed sofa in the sunlit conservatory, and she was surrounded by a menagerie of very healthy looking, active animals and birds. Cats, dogs, parakeets, tortoises, you name it, they were there. Some were in cages, but many were just roaming at will or flying round the house. But the house was spotlessly clean and the animals were clearly well fed, safe, and they appeared delighted to be staying with their benefactor, Mrs. Harmsworth.

Hilary Harmsworth was relieved to see us, and she very quickly showed she was a delightful person. "John," she said, "your mum has told me you like animals. Come and see my seagull that has lived so long with me and my cats. It now thinks it is a cat itself." And there was a seagull that had landed in Hermione's yard when its wing was broken. The seagull was drinking milk out of a saucer, and my memory tells me it was meowing like a cat. Well, in any event it was making an odd sound for a seagull. I had the most wonderful experience that day; and, after she returned from the hospital, I made many return visits to see Mrs. Hilary Harmsworth and her menagerie.

I am sure the Apostles experienced pleasant surprises in their visits, as they spread the good news of Jesus Christ. We will hear next week about the dangers and persecutions they will face during their mission, and the courage they will need to do God's work. I am certain, however, that the goodness of humanity was also revealed to them in their experiences.

As I spent time in Hilary Harmsworth's house almost fifty years ago, I began to understand what it means for a house to be worthy. I found that the Good News of Jesus Christ was already well rooted in that place. As a young man I shook off the dust of my fear and misconception of Hilary Harmsworth. Dear Hilary was truly a gift from God; she used her God given gifts productively. She loved and respected His creation and clearly had devoted much of her life to the welfare of God's creatures.

Let us all listen to God's mission for each of our lives. Let us have the courage of our faith in Lord Jesus to enter into strange houses, to enjoy new experiences and to convey the Good News of Jesus Christ to the world around us. Let us be careful of our preconceptions while being certain in our faith that God loves us, is totally committed to us, and accompanies us on all our journeys through this life.

Be alert to challenges to our Christian values

From the first chapter of The Acts of the Apostles: "Men of Galilee, why do you stand looking up toward heaven? This Jesus who has been taken up from you into heaven, will come in the same way as you saw him go into heaven."

Today's readings have an unusual feature: the first reading in our Lectionary, from the Acts of the Apostles, describes events that occur after the events in the Gospel. Luke, traditionally seen as the author of both books, introduces the book of Acts with a narrative to a certain 'Theophilus', meaning in Latin 'Lover of God'. Theophilus maybe was a Roman official, or other citizen who loved God and who is thought to have been the audience to whom Luke addressed both books.

The body of our Lord Jesus has left us today. The physical body of a young man in his thirties has gone to sit at the right hand of the Father in heaven. But as with the disciples there is no point in our lifting our eyes and gazing toward heaven. We can search in the cosmos for ever; we will only be disappointed.

Even with our sophisticated technology such as the Hubble telescope, scanning the depths of the seemingly eternal universe, still we will not find him. And the reason is quite simple: the body is somewhere quite different; it is in you and in me together. WE are the body of Christ. As Paul writes in Ephesians, "*And God, he has put all things under his feet and has made him the head over all things for the Church, which is his Body, the fullness of him who fills all in all.*"

I think everyone at some time in life has heroes. It is perhaps more common when one is young. I had a hero in my early twenties, and his name was Terry Lake.

My sport of choice while at school in Wales and then in London was rowing. After I graduated from college I joined an independent rowing club in West London and quit only when I left Britain to come to the United States in 1970.

Terry Lake was a successful attorney, but he was also a rowing coach. For those of you that have witnessed a rowing crew in training on the water, Mr. Lake as we called him, was one of those guys on the shore who would cycle down the tow path next to the river Thames, shouting orders through a megaphone at an aspiring team of rowers. Mr. Lake was my coach for two years at Vesta Rowing Club in London. He had won an Olympic medal; he was six feet five inches, an imposing figure and a huge personality. Above all Mr. Lake believed in winning.

Mr. Lake took what was certainly a motley crew of young men from diverse backgrounds, with varying degrees of talent, and molded us into a winning team. He took a squad of ten of us, physically worked us to the bone and despite our own personal doubts, made us winners. We won seven regattas in one year, even beating two well-known American College eights at the famous Henley Royal Regatta in 1969; it seems such a long time ago!

Our Gospel readings since Easter day have gradually led us to this Ascension Day. We have heard the story of doubting Thomas, of believing without seeing. On the road to Emmaus, of Paul's getting it right, finally understanding his true relationship with Jesus. Then we heard our Lord's words, *"I am in the father and the father in me"* and last Sunday, the vine and the branches, that our life flows from the life of God in Christ.

These readings describe what it will be like with the physical Jesus no longer present with us in our lives. We have been prepared to trust in Him, to have faith that Jesus is God and that he will come again and remain with us in the power of the Holy Spirit.

One Friday evening our rowing team arrived at the river Thames for an important training session, but our coach was a no-show.

Mr. Lake was late for the first time in two years. An hour later we heard that Terry Lake had died from a massive heart attack, on his way to be with us.

Vesta Rowing Club appointed an interim coach for our team, a nice guy but no Terry Lake. We were going nowhere. We all felt that the other guy was to blame, and things got worse: two of our best athletes quit the team in disgust. But then our interim coach reminded us in a quiet voice, quite simply, "You must remember that Terry's spirit to win and to excel... lives on in each of you."

A month after Terry's death, our team at Vesta rowing club won again. We won because eight of us, of different sizes, with differing degrees of talent, possessed of different physical strength, rowed and raced as if we were one body, and we were fast, we were confident, and we knew that we could win on our own, because we were really not alone.

So it is with us as Christians. The Body of Christ that is gone, is, in fact, right here. We are not alone, we together are that Body, gathering week by week, hearing scripture, worshipping and praying as one body. Supporting and loving each other as Christ taught us. The body gathered to feed each other and to anoint and lift up our sick and injured. The body gathered to be compassionate and forgiving.

Let us not search the heavens in vain. Christ is with us Emmanuel; we are Christ's body, Christ's Community of Faith.

Spiritual growth nurtured in faith from the spiritual seed

From the 4th Chapter of Mark's Gospel "and the seed would spout and grow, he does not know how."

Earlier in his Gospel, Mark tells us how Jesus taught his disciples about the use of parables in His teaching.

Jesus told his followers that the faithful have been given the secret of the kingdom of God...thus they will understand the implications of the parable stories and will be able to explore the depth and meaning of the parable. But those who do not get it will not comprehend the meaning and thus will not be in a position of being able to ask questions and thus will not reap the benefit of God's word present within the parable...

The word "parable" is from the Latin word 'parabola' meaning comparison. It may be of interest to some of us that the word "parabola" is also derived from the same Latin word parabola.

These days we are constantly reading about the Hubble telescope, and how for the first time human beings can peer deep into the secrets of God's creation, the cosmos. I do not pretend to understand very much at all about Hubble, but I am told that one of the principle techniques used by the telescope is a parabolic mirror that focuses light emissions from the universe so that we can better understand how we fit in to God's physical creation.

Parables in Holy Scripture are the Hubble telescopes of faith and wisdom. Parables and Hubble telescopes both reflect light and truth. Both make it possible for us to see what would otherwise escape our attention. As spiritual telescopes, parables bring the Gospel message into focus and challenge us to peer ever more deeply into the mysteries of life and faith, mysteries that we might never come to without the aid of the parable itself. I believe this is why our Lord loved them so, and employed them so widely in his teaching.

So back to this morning's parable. In just four verses, and only appearing in Mark's Gospel, what is this great truth that the Lord would have us learn from the parable of the growing seed? The seed of course is the word of God and it is inevitable that God's seed will grow when it is received, by faith, into the heart of the hearer. That the word of God grows independently in the heart of the faithful.

I read this past week of how in 1786 William Carey, noted Baptist Reformer, had taken on in his heart the burden of world mission for Christianity. He had laid out his inspiration and plans for this mission before a ministerial meeting in Northampton in England.

The renowned and eminent Rev. Dr. Ryland, who at one time had been William Carey's theology professor, stood to his feet and said to him: "Young man, sit down: when God is pleased to convert the heathens, He will do it without your help or mine."

With the greatest respect to Dr. Ryland I do not believe what he said to be true... there is an inevitable and independent growth of the seed, but there are other contributory factors that God has pre-ordained: the sower must sow, water must be poured on the seed, and the soil must be fertile.

Without these vital ingredients, there will be no harvest of souls in Christ's Kingdom.

My Great Uncle Wilfred lived in North London and was one of the sweetest, kindest people you could meet. I enjoyed visiting him when I worked in the City of London, and Uncle Wilf contributed a lot to my life...among those contributions he taught me how to play cribbage.

Uncle Wilf was a transplant from the English countryside; he grew up in, and would often visit, the county of Wiltshire. On one of his trips he brought back with him a root of asparagus. Now I recall that asparagus did not have a reputation of growing well in the clay soil of North London, but Uncle Wilf persisted and planted the root.

In the Gospel today, Jesus tells us that the sower would sleep and rise night and day, and the seed would sprout and grow, he does not know how.

A couple of weeks went by until I next visited Uncle Wilf. He was very excited and said "John come and see the asparagus'. Well, you could just see one spear appearing through the soil, not more than one half of an inch long. Uncle Wilf's wife, Aunt Ruby, walked by…"the man's finally gone quite mad," she muttered.

In the parable today the Lord is teaching us to be patient. The Word is growing secretly. We may not know how it happens. We may not understand it. Jesus is teaching the great truth that God is at work in the conversion process. It does not depend on us. Once we have done what we have been charged to do, then we are to rest in the fact that God will work.

The next news about the asparagus came in a very worried phone call from my Aunt Ruby. "John…you won't believe it…Wilf has dug up the asparagus to find out why it is growing so slowly". "Boy," I said, "I bet that has made a big difference." "The whole thing is quite ridiculous," came the reply.

In the parable the growth of the seed into a blade, a head, and then the full grain, suggests an appointed order of development that may not be hurried or skipped over, nor can it be delayed. The process of spiritual growth is spontaneous within the kingdom of God, but it remains a total mystery to natural humanity.

About a month later, I was invited by Aunt Ruby to Sunday lunch. When I arrived…Uncle Wilf was visibly elated… "guess what vegetable we are having today"… not too difficult to guess albeit with a hint of surprise. "Yes…asparagus… John, you will love it." I couldn't wait.

Jesus is telling us that growth in faith "will come in God's time and in God's way, not by human effort or in accordance with human logic".

Uncle Wilf passed me the enclosed vegetable dish... I opened it... and there lying alone in this huge bowl was one rather anemic, forlorn asparagus spear... and it could not have been more than three inches long. All I could say was, "Uncle... what do I do if I want a second helping?"

Finally, I see the purpose of today's parable as not to tell us to just sit back and do nothing to promote our Lord's work in the world, but in the work that we are doing for the Kingdom we should remember that it is only God who causes the growth. Whether it is growth in our churches or growth in our personal lives, it is always a mystery, and a miracle brought about by God's grace. God's word has to be planted in us... but we humans have to nurture it. We have to exhibit patience and faith that God will cause his miracle to occur.

We must not doubt God's activity and dig up Uncle Wilf's asparagus root. We also must not doubt God's call to William Carey. Instead we work hard and trust in the Lord... the harvest will surely come.

Be generous with God's unique gifts given to us

"Since there will never cease to be some in need on the earth, I therefore command you, open your hand to the poor and needy neighbor in your land".

The scripture readings selected for today all describe the nature of God's gifts to us.

In Mark's Gospel we heard the story of Jesus raising a child from the dead. Jairus, the girl's father, pleads with Jesus to heal his daughter who lies gravely ill. Jesus is then pulled aside to minister to another of the faithful, but then receives word that Jairus's daughter has died. Jesus asks Jairus to have faith and Jesus gives the ultimate gift - the gift of life.

In his second letter to the Church in Corinth, Paul's objective is that he is fund-raising to support the struggling Church in Jerusalem. Paul hopes the Corinthians will want to be generous, not because of any guilt trip, but because of the model of generosity provided by Jesus. *"For you know the generous act of our Lord Jesus Christ, that though he was rich, yet for your sakes he became poor, so that by his poverty you might become rich."* God's gift to us, Jesus Christ our Lord, taught us that by giving, we receive; that God will provide for us. Our responsibility is to be good stewards for the gifts that he has bestowed on us. Not to question the nature of God's gifts, but to understand what we are given and use the gifts to the very best of our ability because the gifts ultimately are God's gifts. We believe God's gifts are given to us for our use and the work of Christ's kingdom in this life; but at the very most we are stewards of his gifts, not the owners of God's gifts to us.

The Book of Deuteronomy contains three speeches by Moses to the people of Israel. Each of these speeches reaffirms the Covenant between God and the people of Israel.

The word "Deuteronomy" in fact means "the second law". The book is a refresher course for Israel, interpreting the Law into a then-modern context. Scholars see the book of Deuteronomy as a wake-up call for Israel to be attentive to God's gifts and His expectations for the way Israelites conduct their lives.

In today's reading from Deuteronomy we heard about the rules for lending in ancient Israelite Law: that every seven years debts were forgiven, and if the creditor had a lien or other claim against the person owing the money, then that claim was also dismissed. These laws, while difficult to appreciate in our time, proclaim a fundamental principal in Israelite law that the rights and needs of individuals override the rights of property. The law itself arose from the belief that all wealth is a gift of God. People ultimately have no claim over their accumulated wealth: it is God's wealth – once again we are the stewards of God's gifts, not the owners.

In the early 1960s, in Wales, I served an internship studying to become a Chartered Accountant (equivalent to a CPA in the States). The internship is still called "Articles of Clerkship". A remnant from Dickens' time, Articled Clerks were sons (now including daughters) of wealthy or influential parents. Articled clerks back in the 1960s were unpaid and working for the city's premier CPA firm was a privilege. In my case, my dad knew one of the partners, and while it proved an excellent training, it exposed me to a group of guys who spent much of the time talking about how wealthy they were going to be, how many millions they would accumulate and how this would make them masters of their worlds. Two of these young men were a certain Philip and a Thomas. Both of these young men went into somewhat modest, but financially successful family businesses.

In 1998, in a public offering, Philip sold his shares in a retail store for millions of dollars. Thomas was recently named in the top ten most wealthy Welshmen, a family business now worth multimillion dollars.

Every time I read Welsh business news on the Internet, I

read about Thomas and his achievements, his bid to host the golf Ryder Cup golf course, his new "American style" golf course. His company's name blazoned across the front of the Cardiff City soccer club shirts as team sponsor.

There are times when I am envious about Thomas and Philip's accumulation of wealth. Regardless of what I have achieved in my life, I quietly chastise myself that I have not accumulated more money than I have, particularly given my education and other advantages. I undoubtedly covet the influence and prestige that these two guys have back in Wales, in my home. How should I compete with this?

Then I regain a proper perspective. My friends, my family and fellow Christians remind me of the gifts that God has blessed me with in my life. How fortunate and how thankful I am for these gifts!

I truly understand the call for all of us Christians, to use our personal wealth and all our gifts to the benefit of others, and to help Christ's kingdom grow and flourish in this world.

We should not compare the gifts God has given to one person with those given to another. The measure is how we all use God's gifts. It is God's job to judge us, not ours, and we believe we are judged on our own merit, not in comparison with others. It is certainly not our responsibility to judge others as to how they use God's gifts, but it is right for us as Christians to teach other to use our gifts and to follow the rule of life that Jesus taught us.

We may think we have worked hard and deserve the gifts that God has bestowed on us… or we may think we have not worked hard enough and deserve more. Both lines of thinking can only cause trouble for ourselves. We are what we are; we are human beings with human frailties. We all have different obstacles to deal with in our lives. I am certain Jesus expects us only to give life our best shot and to use our gifts to the benefit of those in need. We know we have a loving and caring God who wants only the best for us in our lives. Our loving Jesus doesn't measure us by how much money we have in the bank or what corporate empire we control.

Thousands of years ago Moses relayed God's teaching to the people of Israel: *"Open your hand to the poor and needy in your land."*

Jesus taught us not to be simply aware of God's gifts to us, but rather to understand the implications of our own particular gifts, and to maximize the use of those gifts to the benefit of Christ's Kingdom. Jesus taught us to be good stewards of God's gifts and Jesus taught us to be thankful for the gifts bestowed on us. We are to enjoy the gifts that God has given us, not comparing or resenting others but to recognize that we will all receive by giving... and by giving generously of ourselves to those in need.

The power and glory of compassion

From the twenty third chapter of Saint Luke's Gospel: "Then one of the criminals who was hanged with Jesus said, 'Jesus remember me when you come into your kingdom.'"

Our Lord replied, "Truly I tell you, today you will be with me in Paradise."

Jesus rarely revealed to us his divine authority; rather He chose the way of justice, love, and humility in the brief time he spent with us in this world. But now and then we are given just a few glimpses of His awesome glory.

The stories of his birth hinted at what the writer of the Colossians affirms years later—*"for in him all things in heaven and on earth were created..."* - a glory he had known before—*"he, himself, is before all things."* Another brief glimpse of his glory was the sudden appearance of the Holy Spirit at his Baptism and the words only the privileged few heard, the words from His Father in Heaven: *"You are my Son, the Beloved; with you I am well pleased."*

At another time, an audience of just three chosen disciples were to experience the transfiguration where God's glory was revealed through his son.

And, as we heard today, there is this moment at the crucifixion when Jesus assures the penitent thief of a place with him in Paradise. Even at the time of his own excruciating pain and suffering, our Lord Jesus was not wallowing in his own misery; rather he was still able to think and act only for the needs of others, and in so doing he revealed the nature of His glory by promising the criminal a place in His heavenly kingdom.

Today, at the very end of our Church year, let us hold on to these images of Jesus' glory as we examine ourselves and our own situations, as we take stock of our own attitudes and our performance as Christians in this world. How well do we emulate the behavior that Jesus Christ showed to us? How well do we follow his example in the way we live out our lives?

Some of you may remember my stories that involved my

friend Robert McDermott "Mac" in Wales. Mac the gentle giant, six feet six inches tall was the friend who literally carried me in to school one day when I experienced a sudden asthma attack on the school bus.

When we were both fifteen years old you may remember Mac was my business partner in our failed venture to grow mushrooms. Then just ten years ago Mac and I travelled in a hot air balloon over southern England, the balloon that crash landed in a field, to encounter the irate farmer whose anger only abated when he was given a bottle of gin as a peace offering.

Mac and Shirley McDermott moved to Spain to live in 2005. Shirley McDermott, a four feet six inch rather frail looking Welsh woman, was one of the kindest, most selfless people I have ever met. But our Shirley was also a tough soul. She had no qualms in berating Mac and me about how much beer we used to drink and how overweight we were. I can still hear her voice.

Today is the last Sunday of our Church Year and is also known as the Feast of Christ the King. Christ is King because he is the Son of God. He is both perfect human and perfect God, and because he is God, he is ruler of all that is; sole ruler because God is one. None other is worthy because only the one who created everything has the power of absolute rule over his creation.

Christ is King because he has redeemed all creation, and especially human nature, bringing us the promise of everlasting life and peace. By taking our human nature on himself he restored in us the image of God which we had vandalized by our disobedience and our ability to separate ourselves from God.

By becoming human, and by taking upon himself not only our nature, but the punishment due us for our sins, Christ reconnected us to God thus enabling us to be God-like in our lives. When Shirley and Mac lived in Wales, Shirley was a nurse's aide in a home for physically and mentally challenged young women. One of Shirley's most complex patients was a twenty year old woman, Julie, who lived her life curled up in a ball in the corner of her room and communicated with no one in this life except for Shirley.

The nursing home hit financially hard times and was scheduled to close its doors. And with this closing many of the patients including Julie had literally nowhere to go. These patients were slipping through the cracks in a supposedly watertight care for all, National Health Service. Julie would end up on the streets as one more homeless person.

Mac and Shirley had a minimum of financial resources at the best of times, but despite that, despite the fact that Shirley was about to lose her job, Mac and Shirley made the decision to become legal guardians for Julie. Julie would live with Mac and Shirley for the next ten years.

Today's Gospel depicts Christ the King revealed on the cross in his true Glory. But while suffering for our sins, Jesus' thoughts were not of self-pity, revenge or anger, but rather his thoughts and actions were toward reassuring the repentant thief that he would join our Lord in Heaven.

Jesus' thoughts and actions were those of a selfless, perfect human being as well as being Christ the king, the Son of man in all His Glory.

When I first met Julie, she was huddled in the corner of Mac and Shirley's living room. At first glance she looked like a bundle of rags, as if dumped unceremoniously in a pile in that tiny room. But then she moved and this thin, white little face appeared and smiled at me. She did not say a word, but I could just sense that she felt safe there in that small home with Mac and Shirley.

A couple of years later I arranged to meet Mac and Shirley at a restaurant near their home. Mac and Shirley arrived first and were already seated when I walked into the restaurant. But there was a third person with them, a slim dark haired young woman with a smile that was sort of familiar to me.

"John," Mac said, "I believe you have already met Julie." Julie extended her hand to me and said, "Good evening, Mac and Shirley's friend John from America."

As I write this story I am moved to tears when I remember the feelings of the power of good that had been brought to bear in that home in the care given to Julie by Shirley and Mac. How proud Jesus Christ must be of dear Shirley who died this past year in the Spanish village of Villa Del Mar at her home with Mac, her husband of forty years.

Jesus revealed in his Glory on the Cross, offered forgiveness and life eternal to the repentant thief. Jesus at the moment of his most intense suffering. was not thinking about his own needs, his own welfare. He was instead thinking of the needs of a common criminal.

Shirley and Mac at the moment of their own deep financial troubles, also were not thinking of their own needs, but rather the needs of Julie the helpless, infirmed, illiterate, crippled of body, mind and spirit.

I saw Julie one more time and that was two weeks before her marriage in 1993. Julie went on to become a mother and remained good friends with Mac and Shirley for the rest of Shirley's life

Today on the Feast of Christ the King let us take stock of our kind acts and generous thoughts for those around us in greater need than ourselves.

Let us thank God for this past year in the life of the Church, and let us remember Mac, and his wife, the late Shirley McDermott. Let us give thanks for the life of Julie and her family, and let us thank God for sending His Son our Savior Jesus Christ to show us what it means to love and care for each other.

Humility – truth of self – brings us closer to God

From the Gospel according to Luke, we have just heard the parable of the Pharisee and the tax Collector: "I tell you this man went down to his home justified rather than the other; for all who exalt themselves will be humbled, but all who humble themselves will be exalted."

Humble is a difficult word from a number of perspectives. Firstly I am certain it has a different meaning for each one of us. It is a word that in some ways is better defined by what it is not rather than what it is. Humble is not proud or haughty; humble is not arrogant or overly aggressive. Humble is not self-aggrandizing. Humble is not self-exalting.

Many of you know I like to frame my sermons around a personal story, but I admit to having had some difficulty with a story relevant to today's topic. I needed a story, a story, preferably from my distant past that provided an example of my personal lack of humility.

As I usually do when faced with serious obstacles in life, and after having racked my brain for hours trying to think of an occasion when I displayed any semblance of a lack of humility, I asked my wife Karen, if she could think of a story. Karen thought for maybe three seconds and replied, "How many stories do you want? How about the rowing coach?"

In Luke's Gospel the lack of humility shown by the Pharisee not only distorts his own view of the world, but acts as a barrier in his relationship with God.

The Pharisee's conceit is plain to see: he is proud of himself and his status in the community which may be justified but he allows his ego to get out of control, and in his prayers to God the Pharisee gives thanks that he is not like other mere mortals. He sees himself as clearly superior to the sinners of this world, and definitely superior to that tax collector over there. He gives thanks to God for who he is: he is a Pharisee and he knows that God will look particularly kindly on him.

In the late 1960s, in London, I was very active in the sport of rowing. I represented my high school and local club in eight oar racing and after college was a member of the 'B' squad at the well known Vesta Rowing Club in London. I took this pastime very seriously and our squad trained every day either on the river Thames, or in what seems now to have been an ongoing boot-camp torture of physical fitness programs.

One spring we were out practicing sprint starts in preparation for the Annual Head of the River Thames race, a particularly strenuous time trial over a four and a half mile course.

We had a new coach, 'Tim Fox'. His name is forever emblazoned in my memory. Mr. Fox, as he liked to be called, was in a motor launch following our boat and was intently watching our individual rowing techniques. I remember him even examining the size and depth of the puddles created by our oars as they entered the water, to gauge how hard we were working. This was all a very big deal for us. We were eager to impress him because there were four alternates in our squad who trained with us and were only too ready to take our place if we, individually, were not selected for a race.

At the end of the practice, we rowed slowly toward the clubhouse and stopped. Mr. Fox, a small man with a loud voice, particularly when using a megaphone, proceeded to heap criticism on each of us in turn. I rowed at the number four position in the boat.

Mr. Fox proceeded to criticize each of us in turn, in public there on the river. He started with the bow man, and then number two came under attack, then three. My heart was beating faster and faster, but he passed over me and went on to be particularly critical of number five, then six, seven and the stroke.

Mr. Fox had made no criticism of me as he worked through the boat. I felt so superior, my moment had arrived: cream does rise to the top! I knew I was better than all the other guys. Truth will tell. I felt that I had just won an Olympic Gold Medal.

In Luke's Gospel Jesus said, *"This man"* - meaning the tax collector -. *"went down to his home justified rather than the other."* "Justified" in this context means "acceptable to God" or "right by God". Jesus is saying that the Pharisees' lack of humility is not just an earthly annoyance or nuance of behavior.

Lack of humility is something far more serious, and has dire consequences that go far beyond a social expression of personality limited to this earthly life. It is said that a lack of humility at any level, including pride in our personal piety, makes it difficult to communicate with God because it gets in the way of sincerity as to who we really are.

Back on the Thames River, I basked in the glow of who I really was as an athlete. I had achieved rowing perfection. I deserved this. I had trained as hard as any in our squad; and Mr. Fox by passing over me for criticism had clearly appreciated my talents.

But then Mr. Fox turned in my direction and, raising his megaphone, said in an incredibly loud voice, "As for you, number four, Mr. Dolan, you rowed like a sack of potatoes. In fact a sack of potatoes would likely have put more energy into their performance." I was confused, devastated, and felt no relationship with my crewmates or this crazy new coach.

In our Gospel story, through their ardent prayer it was clearly the intention of both the Pharisee and the tax collector to maintain a strong relationship with God. Faith is the expression of our relationship with God and faith requires prayer. But prayer is best when it is humble, sincere, and persistent. Lack of humility is an obstruction in our communication with God because it distorts reality of self.

We have every right to be proud of our accomplishments in this life. I was a good rower back in the 1960s. I wasn't as good as I thought I was, but with thanks to Mr. Fox and others, I never developed an inflated ego. Rather, I learned a lot about humility.

We have the right to take pride in our skills, but who are we to come before God with a list of our own accomplishments and expect to be elevated in His sight?

Finally, with thanks to the Rev. Nicholas Dyke, we are reminded of Saint Bernard of Clairvaux's book, "The Steps of Humility." Saint Bernard says:
"Number one ... if you pursue the truth of God you come to contemplation;
Secondly... if you pursue the truth of neighbor you come to compassion;
But thirdly if you pursue the truth of self you come to humility... and with humility our prayers and through our prayers... our relationship with God becomes more real, more meaningful."

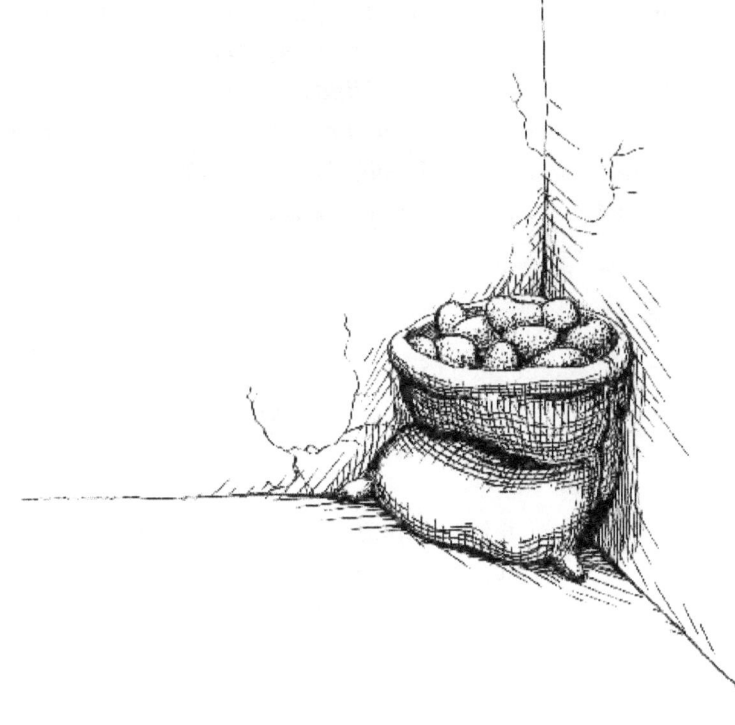

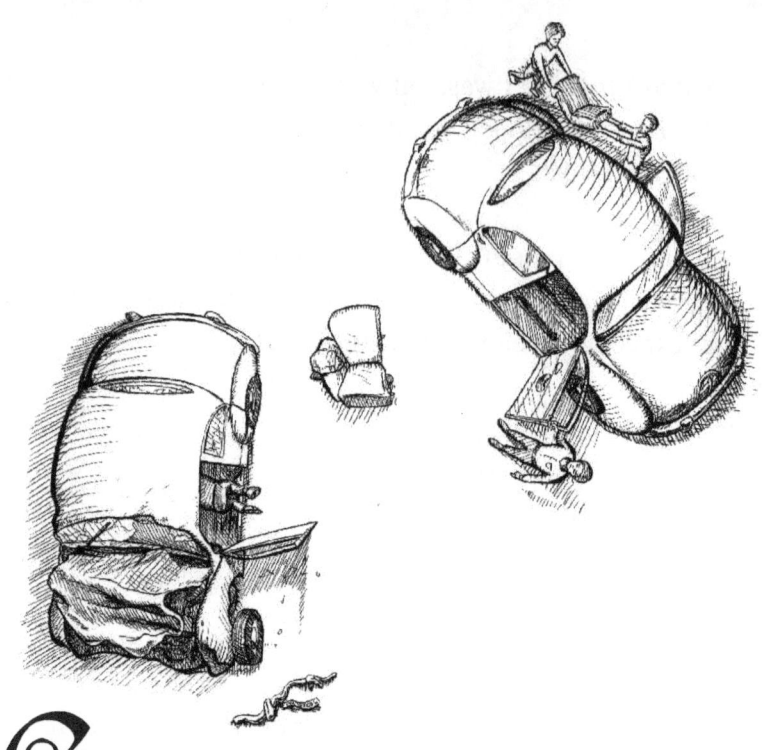

God knows every little detail that lies within our hearts

In today's Gospel Jesus manifests himself as the light of the world. He heals the blind man physically but he does so much more: our Lord opens the blind man's eyes and reveals the wonder and glory of the world. The glory of the world that can only be appreciated through enlightenment when our eyes are truly opened and we realize that our Lord is always with us... active in our lives.

When our eyes are open, then we understand that God loves us, is totally committed to us and whatever our earthly concerns and struggles might be. He is right with us, loving us, forgiving us, holding us in his warm embrace.

As Christians it is imperative that we keep our eyes focused on what is really important in our lives. In spite of the many distractions we face, we must see the real world and the glory of the

Lord. As Christ taught us, we must love God with all our strength; and we must love our neighbors in the same way as we must love ourselves.

We are surrounded by distractions in our everyday lives, and they frequently blur or distort our vision of both our relationship with God and with those we love. The most frequent of these distractions is our human suffering. When we suffer pain, it can feel as if a veil is pulled down over our eyes, whether it be bad health, financial problems, bereavement of a loved one, the desperate feeling of loneliness or disconnection, guilt, abandonment, the pit of depression, addiction. All these distractions can cloud our vision and become obstacles to our relationship with God and our loved ones.

There is not one of us who is immune or protected from the rigors of life; brokenness is a vital part of our human experience.

But the difference for us lies in the redemption of the world through Jesus Christ. Faith in Jesus pierces any veil obscuring our vision of reality, any cloudiness in our vision of the real world around us. Our faith is the answer to any pain and suffering no matter how severe.

Faith in Jesus Christ is the one and only answer. Our beloved Jesus the light of the world is our only remedy.

My dad, Walter Henry Dolan, had strong convictions and he had no hesitation in letting people know that Jesus Christ was at the center of his life. My dad was a discerning man, and you had to get up very early in the morning to pull the wool over his eyes. My dad had 20:20 vision and he had the ability to see Jesus at work in the world. Walter was a highly intelligent, spiritual and mentally strong man. I love my dad and I have missed him very much this past twenty-four years.

St John's Gospel today is all about sight, both physical and spiritual. At the center of the story is the man born blind whose restoration to sight reveals the blindness all around him in the world.

The disciples of Jesus, like us here today, were caught up in the distractions of their own lives, and missed the main event. The religious authorities of the time were also distracted in their lives, in their case by the trappings and impediments of religious tradition. They were so consumed by the fact that Jesus had violated the Sabbath by working a miracle of healing that they also missed the greatest experience the world has ever known: that the Messiah, the Savior of the world, was right there in their midst.

In 1960 Walter Dolan displayed his excellent vision. He decided that his son John needed his own automobile, which was just fine with John. So for the grand sum of $80 my Dad purchased a used sedan from one of the assistant priests from our church in our village in Wales. I was very proud of this vehicle and drove off to college in fine style.

The following Friday evening, when at last we were released from the academic sweatbox, six of us piled into my small car and headed to the local pub. Well, the trip to the pub was fine; but on the way back, suffice it to say I was distracted while driving and we were involved in an accident. The car was so badly damaged that all we could do was push the wreck into a nearby field, and I was forced to abandon my pride and joy.

Thank God that no one was injured, and the six of us walked back to college. But in the face of this near catastrophe only one thought filled my mind: how was I going to tell my dad about the car's demise, without his seeing me as the reckless, irresponsible fool? Which indeed I was by my behavior that night.

In today's Gospel, the blind man's friends and neighbors were distracted by the very act of his healing. This change in the blind man's status confused them and some of them even disowned their friend. His healing had ruptured a social order, and they could not deal with the change.

The friends and neighbors were distracted, and they, like the religious authorities, totally missed the main event, the very presence of Jesus the Messiah, the light of the world. The neighbors and friends were more blind than the beggar before he was healed by Jesus.

Back in my dorm at college I racked my brain; how was I going to get out of this one? My dad was expecting me back for a scheduled vacation in ten days and he would certainly see a problem if I didn't use my car to drive home. I had no money even to buy a train ticket, let alone get the car fixed.

Then I came up with a plan. I would enroll my friends in a fund raising event. I won't go into the details of the fundraising, but suffice it to say the college campus was very close to a famous horse racetrack. With the proceeds I would buy a car of the same model and color; my dad would never notice the difference.

And that is exactly what happened. But there was a snag: a friend pointed out that the outside of the car looked OK but there was a different color of furniture inside the car, and a different license plate number. Oh, dear! Dad will notice the difference the moment he looks inside the car.

Solution: back to the field where I abandoned the car. Transfer old furniture and license plate on to new vehicle. The plan worked like a dream.

Ten days later I was driving home to Wales in this hybrid vehicle. Even Sherlock Holmes would be blindsided, let alone my dad.

This Fourth Sunday in Lent we are called on to acknowledge our own blindness, and to seek Christ's healing touch. But in this seeking of healing there is risk for us. If we truly accept Christ as our savior, if we learn to cope with our distractions by seeing our Lord Jesus, what will happen to us? Will our friends and loved ones still recognize us? How will we deal with the inevitable changes in our vision of life and what is important to us?

On returning home to Wales, my dad asked me how the car was going. I said just fine. Then he said, "Take me for a ride. I have only been in the car one time." I think I turned a grayish-white color and stuttered, "OK, Dad".

My dad loved the drive and was impressed with how well the car ran. I had done it. Pheww. I had hoodwinked my dad even with his wonderful eyesight. I was so proud of myself. I was off the hook. I never mentioned another word about the car thing.

My total lack of vision caused me to be devious, and not to see the unconditional love of my dad for his son, regardless of distractions or circumstances.

In the context of today's Gospel, how does the world look if we allow Christ to heal our blindness, our lack of vision? In Seminarian Don Frye's words from last Sunday, "We will become truly well connected."

We will see God's face in the most unlikely people and places. We will find ourselves evangelizing, filling Emmanuel Church to overflowing. We will hear God speaking through the marginalized, the victimized; and we will see and experience the comfort of our Lord Jesus sharing our pain and suffering with us.

We will understand that God is greater than our worst misfortunes, our misdeeds and all our pain and suffering.

In the story of my dad and the automobile, stay with me as we fast forward twenty years. I was with my dad in the hospital in Wales just three days before he died. This was a special time, and my dad was telling me how much he had loved his dad.

Then in a quiet but firm voice my dad said, "John, regarding the car, you did a good job, but you forgot one detail. The inside roof lining was a different color."

My dad chose to forgive my deception; and I think he knew me for who I really am. How even greater then is God's forgiveness for our misdeeds.

What a privilege it is to have known and loved a man with such clarity of vision as Walter Dolan.

I would like to borrow a sonnet from Robert Burns.

"Oh that some power the gift could give us, to see ourselves as others see us. It would from many a blunder free us and foolish notion."

We pray that our vision be always clear so that we are able to see the presence of Jesus in our lives. When we become distracted, let us regain our sight through the power of our faith, so that we experience the glory of our Lord and Savior, the light of the world.

Take care not to sit in judgment of others; that is God's responsibility

"... Nathaniel replied, 'Rabbi, you are the Son of God! You are the King of Israel.'"

In any movie made of the life of Jesus, Nathaniel would hardly be a leading role. A Mel Gibson or Anthony Hopkins is unlikely to be standing in line, waiting to play this character, because Nathaniel appears just twice in the New Testament, and in only one of the Gospels.

Today's story from John's Gospel is the first mention of Nathaniel in the Bible. It is an important encounter between our Lord and an individual who, prior to meeting Jesus, appears skeptical, living very much immersed in his own narrow view of the world.

The very presence of Jesus immediately opens Nathaniel's eyes to reality. In this brief encounter, he sees Jesus as the Son of God, the King of Israel. No ambivalence or hesitation; Nathaniel sees Jesus as he really is. Nathaniel's belief in Jesus is immediate and uncompromising; he sees life as it really is with our Lord as the center of this world and of life everlasting, the Son of God, the King of Israel.

And with the reality, Jesus gives Nathaniel a promise, a promise of the good news, of "greater things than these," of life everlasting through the love of Jesus Christ.

It was a Friday evening, the rush hour on a London Underground subway train. It was noisy and hot, but by some lucky chance my friend Tony and I managed to get adjacent seats. We were traveling from our college in the City to a suburban apartment. I was tired, and undoubtedly had suffered through the worst week anyone has ever experienced on this planet. Oh, did I have a lot to learn!

I was preoccupied with my personal agenda, and it was somewhat demeaning to be sitting there scrunched together with this heaving mass of mere mortals. In fact as Tony and I sat there looking across at our fellow passengers, a more specific judgment was passing through our minds.

What sort of job do these people have? Why are foreigners taking up seats when good old genuine Londoners are having to stand? In today's vernacular we soon convinced ourselves that we were shut in there that hot Friday evening with a bunch of losers. We just didn't like those people and that was that, a simple agenda, which in turn made us feel different and special.

Jesus described to Nathaniel his premonition of having seen Nathaniel before, under a fig tree, the appropriate place in ancient Judah where Rabbis would sit, study and meditate. An elite spot, maybe.. a place where the student might pass comments on the rest of the world as it passes by, probably. In fact in the verse immediately preceding today's Gospel, when Philip told Nathaniel about Jesus, Nathaniel's immediate comment was, *"Can anything good come out of Nazareth?"* A familiar attitude from another young man two thousand years ago.

But Nathaniel was in for a dramatic awakening when he met Jesus; his myopic view of the world would be changed forever. Nathaniel would see reality; he would see Jesus as our Lord and Savior, the Son of God, the King of Israel. And with the reality, Jesus gives promise. Jesus says to Nathaniel, *"You will see heaven opened and the angels of God ascending and descending upon the Son of Man."*

Back on that hot subway train, some children, apparently with an older man that Tony and I presumed to be their father, were making a lot of noise. "Some parent," we said to each other. "What chance have those kids got in life when they get no direction?" What a perfect target for our criticism. The kids got more rowdy, even knocking over Tony's briefcase.

"That's enough. I am going to tell their dad. Why should we have to put up with this ?" Boy, the moral high ground sure felt great. I stood up and approached the dad, who was sitting quietly in a corner seat.

I proceeded to admonish him for the kids' behavior, and it felt good. It felt even better because I knew I was in the right!

The man looked up at me, and there were tears in his eyes.

"I am so sorry," he said, " we are just returning from the hospital. Their Mom, my wife Nora, died this afternoon. The kids just can't believe it; they are all wound up. I'm sorry about the noise; we will be getting off at the next station."

I was dumbdfounded. I didn't know what to do or say. I just mumbled, "I am so sorry." I looked across at my friend Tony. His head was bowed and his face appeared ashen gray.

Reality broke through at that moment for John and his friend Tony. In an instant we came face to face with the real world, and I saw Christ's face in that father's eyes. Our myopic view of the world based on our own agenda was shattered. I know I was never quite the same after that encounter; I know I encountered Jesus that day.

When Jesus revealed the true world to Nathaniel, that Christ was the Son of God, Jesus promised Nathaniel, *"You will see greater things than these."*

Nathaniel lived to see God's promise, Nathaniel of Cana was one of the disciples to whom the resurrected Jesus appeared on the shore of the sea of Galilee.

Let us all remain connected to the real world as revealed to Nathaniel, John and Tony. Let us live in the warmth of God's promise and love as revealed to us by our Lord Jesus Christ.

Faith in God will heal any human condition

"When Jesus saw their faith he said to the paralytic, 'Son, your sins are forgiven.'"

Jesus was on his first preaching tour in Galilee and the crowds were flocking. He was the hottest act in town, and this level of attention so early in his ministry was of great concern to him. He needed time to do his work, and this level of attention would soon be a threat to the established religious authorities. Last Sunday we heard how Jesus sternly charged the cleansed leper to keep his mouth shut, but of course the leper immediately went out and told everyone he knew that this Jesus of Nazareth had cured him.

So Jesus needed a time out, a brief sojourn in the country

to let things quiet down and let his story at least get off the front page of the "Galilean Tribune." Jesus resumed his tour on the north shore of the Sea of Galilee in the town of Capernaum, but there was still no relief from the crowds, the fans of Jesus the preacher and Jesus the healer.

It is said that there were a group of five construction workers in Capernaum that had been inseparable friends since early childhood. One day the almost inevitable accident occurred: one of this small community of friends fell from a rooftop and was paralyzed. From the time of the accident the four workmates had looked after their unfortunate colleague; they were totally committed to their friend, and would do whatever it takes to make his life more bearable.

This commitment brought them one day to the edge of a large crowd surrounding the house where Jesus was. They had heard about Jesus and it really didn't matter to them whether Jesus was who he proclaimed to be. This was one more way they would try to bring their friend's plight to God's attention; their faith was in the power of God's healing and that God would eventually respond to them.

When the five arrived at Jesus' house, there was just no way of getting through the crowd to gain Jesus' attention, but there was no doubt or hesitation, their friend was going to see Jesus that day. They decided to employ the skills of their trade. They scaled the walls of the house and removing the tile and rafters, made an opening large enough to lower the stretcher down near where Jesus was standing. They captured Jesus' attention, and the Son of God, through their faith, healed their friend.

In August of 1970 there was a huge rock concert on the Isle

of Wight, off the south coast of England. It was the British equivalent of Woodstock, and it attracted huge crowds; some say close to 100,000 people surrounded the open-air stage. I was at college in London, and while I hardly called myself a hippie, nonetheless I found myself and a group of friends standing on a hill, overlooking the concert area, marveling at the spectacle, but as seen through a pair of binoculars.

The concert had already heard performances from stars such as Joan Baez, Donovan etc., but a number of big stars including Jimi Hendrix were already some two hours late arriving, and anyway there seemed no way they would ever get through the crowd to the stage even if they did arrive.

But the fans believed in their rock stars, and everyone we talked to had every faith that they somehow would arrive. The crowd had grown even larger; they were packed around the stage with no way in.

Suddenly we heard the sound of an approaching helicopter, and an army helicopter appeared over the brow of the hill and landed some fifty yards from where we were standing.

The down draft of the helicopter's rotors caused the crowd to scatter, leaving an open path to the stage. Then to my amazement, and thirty years later to the disbelief of our kids, a host of stars emerged from the helicopter. I remember seeing Jimi Hendrix, the Who, and Richie Havens, with their heads down to protect themselves from the wind, walking through the break in the crowd and onto the stage, to a reception the like of which I have never heard since. The faith of that community of fans to the appearance of their rock stars thirty years ago on the Isle of Wight was well justified.
We here this morning belong to a community that is commit-

ted to each other, that is Christ's Community of Faith. When we pray for each other's needs, we as a community bring those needs to God's attention.

Those rock fans on the Isle of Wight, so many years ago, firmly believed that their stars would appear for them and they were not disappointed. How much greater then, is our faith in God, that he will be there for us and that when we bring someone we love to our Lord in faith, that God will hear and respond to our prayers? By acting as one voice as a community we facilitate the opportunity for God's healing. Our commitment to each other and our faith in Jesus requests God's attention, and He will always be there for us.

We know so well from personal experience that the healing does not always bring a physical cure. But there will always be God's healing. The healing of damaged relationships, the release from physical pain through the death of a loved one, the healing of sin, the relief in one's heart when one realizes that one's sins have truly been forgiven.

In the same way that the hippies and rock fans on the Isle of Wight had total faith that their pop idols would somehow make their way through the huge crowd, so the faith of the four friends in Capernaum resulted in their friend's being healed.

We take our friends and loved ones to Jesus in the faith that through Him God will heal our paralysis so that we may live our lives in health and wholeness to love and serve the Lord.

God's "club" is open to all people

From the Acts of the Apostles: "For so the Lord has commanded us, saying, 'I have set you to be a light for the Gentiles, that you may bring salvation to the uttermost ends of the earth.'"

And from the Gospel according to John: "Jesus said, 'A new commandment I give to you, that you love one another; even as I have loved you, that you also love one another.'"

In the early 1970s, shortly after I arrived in this country, the company I worked for sent me on a business trip to Washington DC. It was a beautiful clear day and the plane flew in low over the city toward what was then called National Airport. I looked toward the north, and saw, perched on a hill, an enormous white English style church. The sight was quite surreal: it was as if an English cathedral had been transplanted right out of the old world into the new. I asked one of my fellow passengers what the church was, and he said that it was the then-recently-completed Episcopal National Cathedral.

I remember great feelings of pride coming over me. In my naiveté, I thought, "Not only is the Anglican Church the superior church in Britain, but its influence is so great that it has become the National Church of the USA! And there on that hill shining in the sun is the structure that proves it!"

My experience while attending a service at the same Washington Cathedral the following Sunday underscored my feelings: the liturgy was just like being back at my home church, Llandaff Cathedral. After the service, sitting in the rose garden on the south side of the Cathedral, listening to the change ringing of the bells, I could be home in Wales. The only difference was it wasn't raining in Washington DC. that beautiful spring morning.

My feelings were of what a wonderful world-wide powerful organization I belonged to. As Anglicans we had the grandest churches, the best liturgy, the finest traditional music, mighty organs, colorful robes and processions, our Book of Common Prayer... I was certain the rest of the world just wished they could share in what I had experienced in my Church in my life.

What I was really saying to myself, all those years ago, was what a wonderful, exclusive club I belonged to. It was the simplest of facts: Anglicans had just got it right; and I was dead certain that other Christians just wished they could know our traditions and belong to our club. Other denominations must know deep down they had got it wrong.

But then, on the other hand, did we really want the whole of Christianity invading our Anglican territory? That would involve that unpleasant word "change", a word that at best was despised where I came from, if the word even appeared in the dictionary. In retrospect I was a well-established elitist in those days.

How exclusive and limited was my thinking all those years ago! But through God's good Grace how much, hopefully, my attitude has been transformed in the past thirty some years.

Today we heard Paul and Barnabas describe God's commandment in the reading from the Acts of the Apostles: Christ's Kingdom must extend to the uttermost parts of the earth.

And as described in John's Gospel, Jesus taught us the power and importance of love. Love is the greatest bond that connects us in our personal relationship with God through our Lord Jesus and with each other. We Christians must embrace all people in love in the same way that Jesus loves all humanity - no exceptions - however hard we humans try to create a pecking order.

It is the message and example of God's love that will enable Jesus' message to be accepted by people throughout the world.

In our own lives it is easy to think of ourselves as something special, something unique, something a little better than others. That is the root of elitism in the world. The word elitism denotes that a segment of society or individual perceives itself to be superior to another. This may be based on skills, or the retention of personal power. Elitism may be based on a perceived superior level of sophistication, of the places where we live; it may be based on race or sexual preference. It is often based on education, what schools we went to, but usually it boils down to comparative wealth, to money, often accompanied by the fear or suspicion of another who is different from oneself.

Jesus understood human weakness including elitism. How much easier it would have been for Him to limit His message to the Jewish Community, giving deference to the elite in Jewish society, the Pharisees, the Saducees and others representing the great symbols of the Hebrew tradition. But that was not God's plan, and the Lamb of God understood that plan.

That is exactly why Jesus traveled and taught in cities such as Tyre and Sidon where the majority of residents were Gentiles. Jesus understood that God's plan extended to the uttermost parts of the world; and he understood that it is the power of love that will make the difference to people's lives.

Jesus' message transcends elitism in this world. Christ's message of salvation is directed to the whole world. It is a message that has no bias, no geographic, economic or cultural limitations. The Good News of the love of God and the salvation of the world through the resurrection of Jesus Christ is intended for all of humanity.

Jesus' teachings are not limited or exclusive in any way. They are directed to the whole world; and the way for us to remain connected to Him and not fall into the trap of elitism is simply to love one another in the way that God loves each one of us.

To love all our neighbors is not always easy! We are human beings; we all have our obstacles to overcome. We live to a great extent depending on perception and hearsay.

It is hard to love the perpetrators of the evil in Iraq's prisons. It is hard for us to love those who we perceive as not living a good Christian life or less than us in some way. It is hard to love those who engage in what we perceive as elitist behavior, particularly when the behavior has a negative impact on ourselves or our loved ones. It is particularly hard to love elitists when they prove to be our very selves. Many of us experience the fact that the hardest form of love is to love ourselves, because we know all our weaknesses better than anyone else.

Jesus commanded us to love one another as He loves us, no exceptions, no excuses; and Jesus also commanded us to love ourselves. If God can love us entirely and completely then we have no basis, no reason not to love ourselves.

Jesus commanded us to take His Christian message of love and salvation to the uttermost parts of the earth. Let us abandon exclusiveness. Let the doors be thrown open to all people, and let us share with them the Good News of Jesus Christ.

Through openness and humility we are best able to see Jesus Christ at work in our lives

"Jesus said, 'I thank you, Father, Lord of heaven and earth, because you have hidden these things from the wise and intelligent and have revealed them to infants.'"

In Matthew's Gospel we hear Jesus describing his special relationship with God. Jesus tells us of the Good News, that this loving relationship with our Father in heaven through his son our Lord Jesus Christ can also be available to each and every one of us… so long as we can be sufficiently open and humble in our acceptance of this dramatic change in our lives.

Jesus tells us the degree of openness and humility that we need to accept for this relationship with God, is more often found in a child than a "wise and intelligent" adult. Adults on their way to becoming wise and intelligent, become influenced by the world; adults have a bias to what they think they already know. Adults have many of the answers, and we are often fooled into thinking that we are in control. A child is not that smart yet!

The decision to accept Jesus Christ as our Savior involves a recognition of our human powerlessness. We are required to surrender control to Jesus, and for so many of us that can be such a difficult experience, and one that we have to learn over and over again.

In the secular world, my work frequently causes me to drive south on Interstate 57. One of the few scenic highlights on this journey, unless one has a particular fascination with a hundred varieties of corn and soybeans, is crossing the Kankakee River, a large expanse of tranquil water and in the summer months, swarming with boats of all sizes. A couple of summers ago I had seen a sign near the bridge offering canoes for rent. Great idea! I would ask my wife Karen if she would like to give it a try!

The next weekend found Karen and me gently paddling down the Kankakee River. It felt good. The boat was gliding along; the sun was shining on the water. It felt good to be in control, and Karen and I were proving to be a good team in the canoe paddling business.

As I anticipated, this canoeing thing was going to be easy, and I had been proved right once again. There was clearly no need to read the book, 'The Essentials of River Canoeing', as proposed by my dear wife. In retrospect I showed a remarkable lack of both humility and openness to the essentials of canoeing.

Jesus understood that the two characteristics, humility and openness, are available in infants that make them so much more receptive to new ideas and relationships compared with adults burdened by lifetimes of experience.

The word humility, from the Latin 'humilis', is defined as low, not proud or haughty, not arrogant or assertive, unpretentious, or deferent to. Openness is defined as "not closed or obstructed".

Children are humble by their very nature. That is, they have very little power over their own lives. Children are also open and receptive to new ideas, but they like clarity in those ideas, no fluff: they love the essentials.

Jesus understood that it is not possible for us to lead Christian lives without our being enabled with the characteristics of humility and openness. But he also was a human being in all respects. He knew how difficult it is for us not to try to control things. He was aware that our human knowledge and wisdom can be an impediment and get in the way of our acceptance of our relationship with God. This is simply because most of us travel with a lot of baggage, resulting from our human experience.

Back on the Kankakee River, it was toward the end of our three hours of canoe rental time, and we were headed leisurely back across the river to the dock. However, the canoe suddenly started to gather speed, without either of us paddling! In the space of a couple of seconds we were past the dock and heading downriver. My wife Karen shouted, "I think we had better paddle backwards, right now!" Being a dutiful husband I paddled backwards just as fast as I could. The canoe slowed. My wife then stopped paddling and turned around to face me. In order to hear what she was about to say, I also stopped paddling. "Why weren't you paddling like I said?" she asked.

At that moment I have never felt so out of control in my whole life. I was sweating, near exhaustion from paddling backwards, only to be shouted at by my wife for not paddling. And as for the canoe... we were now heading at breakneck speed for a bunch of jagged rocks. There was a sickening crunch; the canoe lurched. We had gone aground on the rocks.

In the midst of this trauma, one positive thought flashed through my mind: the only saving grace about this experience was at least nobody saw us.

Then, horror upon horror, I looked over at the river bank. The owner of the canoe rental company was not only watching this whole spectacle through a pair of binoculars, he was preparing to wade out and pull us ashore. It turned out the Kankakee River is no more than two feet deep at that point! Humility? That afternoon I earned a Ph.D. in humility.

We all have experiences when our lives are out of control, usually because we think we know everything and close our minds to new ideas. As Christians those are the times when we must remember and be open to our loving relationship with God through the Good News of our Lord and Savior Jesus Christ. We must remember that Jesus is there for us at all times... whether we are paddling along without a care in the world, whether we are caught up in a maelstrom or stranded on jagged rocks.

Possessed with the characteristics of humility and openness, we are prepared and able to recognize and be safe in the presence of our Lord Jesus.

Christ's promise of peace and true safety

"Do not let your hearts be troubled, and do not let them be afraid. Christ lives within us."

Today's Gospel story is sometimes called 'the promise of peace'. As we approach the Feast of Ascension and then Pentecost, we are reminded that Jesus spoke very clearly of the Holy Spirit. In fact there are five passages between chapters 14 and 16 of St John's Gospel that talk to the ministry of the Holy Spirit.

But first things first. Before we proceed with the homily I would like to wish a Happy Mothers' day to all, but particularly to all the Moms in our community both living and deceased. God bless you all for your enduring love and protection, your generosity, and from my life experience, your incredible patience.

In the original Greek, the Holy Spirit is described using the noun Parakletos, referring to one who is called upon to intercede in behalf of, or to help someone. In the King James Version we hear Parakletos translated as "the Comforter", other times "Counselor" and in our version today "Advocate".

Many of us find language to be so inadequate to reflect feelings. In today's Gospel, Jesus is preparing those who love him for the inevitable, that He will be leaving them as a physically recognizable being. But, at his request, our Father in heaven will provide a Parakletos, an Advocate to be with them, to show them all things and to be with them for all time.

Jesus is describing the incredible gift of the Holy Spirit, but I am certain that the disciples' reaction was simply one of horror that their Lord and Master would no longer be with them.

How could the disciples be expected to understand the awesome nature of the Holy Spirit, that God the Father will save them even from the worst disaster imaginable, that of losing their beloved Jesus? I am sure the disciples were consumed at the thought that Jesus was going to die.

About twenty years ago the Dolan family spent two wonderful weeks on the island of Cozumel. Our daughter Michelle was twelve years old and our son David, ten. There cannot be many places in the world where the water is more inviting, and the four of us to this day are strong swimmers.

One morning David and I were swimming together about one hundred yards off the coast. Periodically both of us went under the water to view the thousands of multicolored fish. All the colors of the rainbow, the sun on our faces, swimming close to my son; it was one of those precious moments when you wish you could freeze time... simply wonderful.

I am certain the time spent with Jesus of Nazareth was a wonderful experience for his disciples. We love Jesus, and that comes from what we are told about him. Just imagine how the disciples felt about our Lord. It had to be the most amazing time of their lives…a time full of love, of righteous teachings. Hearing the good news that God loves us and cares for us. Witnessing Jesus healing the sick, supporting the poor and needy. Confronting greed and evil in the world. The disciples must have been overwhelmed by the goodness of this man Jesus.

And now they were told that he was going to leave them. Just imagine how they felt; they probably didn't even hear the description of the Holy Spirit, let alone understand that the Spirit would always be there to defend and to comfort them in their time of need.

Back in Cozumel, in that deep blue water, David and I suddenly felt a strong undertow pulling us out from the shore. I shouted to Dave for us to swim back to the shore because we were being dragged out to sea. I then put my head down into the water and struck out toward the shore.

What seemed as just a few seconds later I looked up and I was even further out from the shore. So I looked around for David. He was nowhere to be seen. I cannot describe the absolute terror I felt at that moment. My son had disappeared from my view and I was being dragged out further and further toward the open sea.

I screamed and waved my arms to the shore hoping that someone on the beach would see me and help me in some way. I was terrified.

I interpret today's Gospel as telling us that Jesus clearly recognized the disciples' feelings at the prospect of losing him. *"Peace I leave with you; my peace I give to you. Do not let your hearts be troubled, and do not let them be afraid."*

As the screenwriter and director Billy Wilder described it, "Hindsight is always twenty-twenty." We of course understand what is going to happen next when the risen Jesus ascends to heaven. God the father will provide us the Holy Spirit to be our Paraclete, our Comforter, our Counselor, our Advocate. Christ in God will be with us Emmanuel.

In Cozumel, someone on the beach saw this man struggling in the strong current. Within minutes a rescue boat was alongside me. An onboard paramedic was checking me out, but all I could do was shout at them, "My son is missing! My son is missing!"

I was terrified. I had put my son in danger. a ten year old boy faced with that strong current. What was wrong with me to do that?

My rescuers knew nothing about any young boy being in similar trouble in the water. They had only seen me out there. I was the one that was in mortal danger, because not only was there the strong undertow but there were dangerous rocks close to where I was swimming. Seconds later we arrived back at the beach. I felt sick and totally desperate.

John the Evangelist describes how Jesus speaks of his absence and departure that gave rise to the disciples' feelings of great loss. But Jesus promises his friends the gift of the

Spirit, the promise of a new kind of holiness…the promise of peace and safety that will come into their, and our lives. John describes a divine presence that the Holy Spirit will reveal to them.

There is a slang expression in "English" English that best describes my reaction when I got out of the rescue boat on the beach at Cozumel. I was "gob smacked"; I was dumbstruck. There standing on the beach was my son David. In response to my, "What on earth are you doing here?" David explained that he swam underwater and used the rocks to help pull himself back to the shore. He got back to the beach in minutes and then was looking for me. It was David, my ten year old son, who saw me apparently in difficulty and requested the rescue party take the boat out.

As Christians, as we accept and understand the promise that Jesus describes in today's Gospel, our lives are enriched. We grow into the fullness of a relationship with God that never dies.

The real truth is that it was my son David who really saved my life that day in Cozumel. In the same way that the feeling of terror at the prospect of losing someone I love so dearly was replaced by peace and fulfillment, so it is with the departure, the absence of the physical Jesus Christ.

The void left by the departure of the living Jesus is filled with the power and richness of God in the form of the Holy Spirit.

As we enter into a true relationship with the risen Christ, as we open our hearts to the real truth revealed in the power of the Spirit, we realize Christ's promise of peace, of true safety, of fulfillment and joy in our lives.

Presenting ourselves at the Lord's table, just as we are

"...the one who eats this bread will live forever."

Many of us remember that in the 1950s the evening meal was still very much a family affair. I am told this was the case in suburban America and it was also true for the Dolan family home in Wales.

In my parents' home in Wales, the oversize square dining table in the small dining room resulted in a cozy setting indeed. But with four strong personalities, my Mum Joan, my Dad Walter, sister Lizzie and me, that dining table was also the focal point for many and varied agendas, not all discussions reaching peaceful conclusions!

Every day the evening meal had a different focus. Every day was different. Jokes... galore, chastisement... plenty. Frustration and tiredness from the day's hectic agendas, an

A+ in English, a new boyfriend. Friendly (?) competition between siblings. Tensions, joy, unfulfilled ambitions, successes, jealousies, sickness, you name it, we had it. Four strong personalities, a loving family, yes, but a busy table.

That dinner table in Llandaff, Wales in the '50s was a very central place in our lives. It was always a place filled with food, but it was also a table filled with extraneous baggage and distractions. It was too complicated a place, and frequently it was a place I left feeling hungry and empty inside!

Today's lessons describe the Eucharist as the very center of our lives of faith: that the one who eats the Bread of Life will live forever. We are reminded that as we eat the Body of Christ and drink His Blood that we experience Blessed Redemption and newness of Life as if for the first time.

We are reminded that we should come to the Eucharistic table, simple, just as we are. To check our personal baggage at the door and come to our Lord's Table with our hearts and minds open to new experiences, receptive to a renewed relationship with each other in our Christian family and with God.

In the Book of Proverbs, Lady Wisdom invites us to the table for a banquet, but even though it is a banquet, the table is set for the simple, the uncomplicated and unencumbered: To taste life in the bread and wine, to lay aside immaturity and live in a life of insight.

In St. Paul's letter to the Ephesians we are cautioned as to the pitfalls of excess in food and drink: that the Eucharist is not a time for self-centered agendas, but a time to be open to the Will of God.

John's Gospel explains the mystery of the person of Jesus in a way not seen in the Synoptic Gospels; the Evangelist author records the real events, but then uses their own interpretation to a much greater extent, including many terms of everyday life to make the significance of Christ both clear and gripping.

Bread, water, light, life; words that are fundamental and central to our lives here on earth are used frequently throughout John's Gospel as symbols to powerfully describe our Lord's teachings.

In July 1997 we were together at the same dining table in Llandaff, Wales. A family dinner now has my wife Karen in my Dad's seat, the rest of us in the same seats that we occupied more than forty years ago. But things are very different. We are here simply to be together with my Mum, who has terminal cancer at the time of this writing.

The dining table is still filled with food, albeit now forty years later with the odd glass of wine or gin and tonic. But there are other major differences. Our baggage is left in our rooms, or checked at the door along with our agendas, our successes and failures, our experiences and qualifications.

We are here at this table simply because we want to be... just ourselves, uncomplicated. Simple people wanting to be together to do what we can for our Mum. John's Gospel and its use of everyday words in unfamiliar contexts raises questions for us. What does it really mean to eat Jesus flesh and to drink his blood? Surely it means to become one in Community with each other and with God. How does one reconcile that with a society that stresses so much the rights and responsibilities of the individual?

In a world of fast food and pizza delivery, the 1950s are long gone. Who has the time to spend time at the table with one's own family, let alone with our Lord Jesus?

These questions are answered for us in the Eucharistic sacrifice. We come to our Lord's Table as simple human beings with no expectations but with faith and hope. We are willing to lose "ourselves" to partake in the marvelous abundance of life eternal.

I sat down at that family dining table just four weeks ago in Wales with little or no expectations. I left the table filled with an abundance of love and fellowship with each other and with a sense of a very real closeness with our Lord Jesus.

Through our family's suffering and endurance together we are experiencing a growing closeness with each other and with our Lord that reveals itself even in the midst of the suffering and chaos... truly a Eucharistic experience.

As we partake in our Lord's abundance at the Eucharist this morning, let us leave our personal baggage and agendas in the pews. Let us be open to our Lord's fellowship at our table and with joy look forward to the heavenly banquet in life everlasting... *"the one who eats this bread will live forever."*

Be still and feel God's presence

"And I will ask the Father and He will give you another Advocate, to be with you forever."

Most preachers have favorite reference sources they use to prepare their sermons. There is of course the scripture itself, but there are also numerous Internet-based and published commentaries that can sometimes help us to provide clues toward God's real message embedded in our human words. The resources also help us to be sensitive to the fullness of the message that God is conveying through us.

Well, this week my usual reference materials let me down. The commentaries I normally use invariably focused on the Book of Acts and the encounter between Philip and the royal officer in the Ethiopian court.

The Holy Spirit is mentioned but more in the context of the Spirit working in the conversion of the Eunuch. A powerful story indeed but not the subject I wished to preach on today, the nature of the Holy Spirit.

Even though we are in the Easter season the events in today's Gospel from John occur before the death and resurrection of our Lord. Jesus is foretelling what will happen when He leaves this world. He is preparing his followers for a life without the physical presence of Jesus.

Jesus describes the Holy Spirit as the Spirit of Truth. He describes the sense of the spirit as the promise of an advocate guiding us and dwelling in us.

But why the word advocate? The original Greek translation for Holy Spirit used the noun "parakletos" formed from the verb parakleo "to encourage", or "to exhort".

I looked at five translations of the Bible and found four different words to describe the Holy Spirit. The King James Version uses "Comforter", the New International and Revised Standard Versions the word "Counselor". In The Spirit-Filled Truth Bible the Holy Spirit is the "Helper" and finally the New Revised Standard Version uses the word "Advocate" which confuses things even more since the word 'advocate' is used in the first letter of John as a term describing Jesus Himself.

Oh dear, we human beings do make things so very complicated. The Holy Spirit is with us as an integral part of our daily life of faith and we can't even choose a word to describe it.

When my sermon resources fail me I sometimes turn to the writings of St. Augustine, fourth century Bishop of Hippo in North Africa. Augustine has an inordinate ability to display his down to earth humanness. He cuts to the chase, to zero in on the human implications of Christ's teachings.

St Augustine's famous works, 'The Confessions', and 'The City of God', describe how Augustine spent much of his life torn between the physical pleasures of being just another human being, and the structure and discipline required if he became a Christian. Finally Augustine is converted and becomes one of the great Saints of the early Church. St. Augustine is well qualified to provide a human perspective on the more complex issues within Christianity such as the nature of the Holy Spirit.

And what does St. Augustine say? In the context of both the Blessed Trinity and the nature of the Holy Spirit Augustine writes: "In no other subject is the danger of erring so great, or the progress so difficult, or the fruit of a careful study so appreciable." Well, that's a great help!!! But then I read on ... and once again Augustine comes through.

One of St. Augustine's reflections is entitled "The Holy Spirit, Gift of God's love." It reads as follows: The Holy Spirit- there is no gift of God more excellent than this... Love therefore which is of God and is God, is especially the Holy Spirit, by whom the love of God is shed abroad in our hearts, by which love the whole trinity dwells within us. The Holy Spirit, although he is God Himself, is called also 'the Gift of God'. And by that gift what else can properly be understood except love.

Now we are really getting somewhere with this message for today. But then I start fretting again...

As many of you know I love to tell stories in my homilies to demonstrate the point I am making. I didn't have one today and I felt bad about it, but then I realized (or should I rather say someone realized for me), of course I do: the very journey of preparing this sermon is today's story, and it is a story of the spirit working in our lives.

My wife Karen's mom, Dorothy, was well known for her faithful discipline of daily prayer and Christian reading. On a couple of occasions Karen and I have come across a reflection tucked away in her Bible or other safe place. As I became frustrated with preparing this particular sermon a piece of paper fell out of her Bible and fluttered to the ground under my desk. The piece of paper is a reading from the Daily Word dated November 13, 1996, two years prior to Dorothy's death. The reading provides a fitting description of the Holy Spirit and the comfort and support it brings to our lives.

The reading is entitled: *"I gently still my thoughts and experience the loving presence of God"*.

'I may not know what the future holds for me, but I do know that in the unknown something familiar is waiting for me: God... is always there. Wherever I go, whatever

I do, God's Spirit is within me and goes before me.
By stilling my thoughts and feeling the loving presence of God, I quell any fears of the unknown.
God will never forsake me; God is powerful enough to have created the sun, the moon and the stars of the universe. That same God is still gentle enough to have created the delicate petals of a fragile flower and loving enough to have created me.
As I feel the loving presence of the Holy Spirit I just feel awed. I feel blessed and perfectly safe when I consider that I myself am part of all that God has created.'

The conclusion to this story is... God is love and God requires that we love Him and each other. God's Gift of Himself as the Holy Spirit is a gift of love that we may have a companion, a guide, someone to encourage and exhort us to a faithful life. A helper, a comforter, a counselor and an advocate to be with us forever.

We thank God for His loving kindness to have given of Himself through His Son our Lord Jesus Christ and provided us with the precious gift of love in the Holy Spirit.

Hunger after the really important things in life

For a week in 1997 my family, that is my wife Karen, our daughter Michelle, son David and myself spent a week in northern Michigan, in a tiny rustic cabin on the shores of Lake Superior.

When I say tiny, I mean tiny, the size maybe of a one car garage. Rustic? Well, we did have a shower and a stove. Michelle summed it up really well. "Dad, you have to understand..this is camping..but with a wooden hut instead of a tent."

That made me feel so much better... not! The hunger for a Jacuzzi, a King size bed, swimming pool, gourmet restaurants and all the other luxuries associated with vacations immediately disappeared, NOT. I was now transformed; well adjusted to a simple life for a week on the shores of

Lake Superior, definitely not! However, I was in for a surprise; for a while I was blessed with a much improved, albeit Spartan, perspective. But very soon the hunger for the comforts of life came sneaking back.

The crowd that chased after Jesus was also still hungry, even after an unexpected, free, lavish meal. They had not had their fill; they wanted more from Jesus. More bread and more fish and definitely more of the creature comforts that this man from Galilee seemed to provide so effortlessly, and so abundantly.

But Jesus then rebuked the crowd, *"You are not looking for me because you saw signs, but because you ate your fill of the loaves."* It is as if Jesus said, "You can't think about your souls, because you can't get beyond thinking about your stomachs." That is, of course, exactly what Jesus was saying. Jesus rebuked the crowd for having the wrong perspective, for searching for the wrong thing to satisfy their hunger. They had received the loaves and fishes as mere physical sustenance; they had failed to see the meal as a gift from God.

The Dolans continued to encounter physical hunger during their week on the wild side in Northern Michigan. No access to a telephone, the telephone seen by some of the younger members of our family as the vital daily lifeline to friends and community. The telephone seen by other members of the family, the older ones, as a frequent, noisy intrusion on one's private time.

No television, no White Sox or MTV. Not just no choice of movie, but no movies period!!! No stereo, whether it be "Jimi Hendrix" or "Beethoven". All in all the deprivation of creature comforts was a shock to all the Dolan family members. Creature comforts that are nice to have in life, but hardly essential.

My sense is that the crowd that pursued Jesus across the lake were not concerned with anything too much beyond their superficial physical hunger. But they were quickly reminded by our Lord of the other real hungers in life, spiritual hungers that can only be satisfied by a full, unconditional relationship with God.

We have a hunger for truth; Jesus alone can provide that truth. We have the hunger for life; Jesus alone can give life its real meaning. And there is the hunger for love. Jesus alone can give to humanity the love that outlasts sin and death.

It is only our Lord Jesus Christ who can satisfy the immortal longings and the insatiable hunger of the human heart and soul.

In the space of just a few days, the new day settlers, the Dolans in their rustic cabin on the shores of Lake Superior, had become reasonably well adjusted to their surroundings. Joining in their neighbors' nightly campfires. Learning how the locals survived the frigid winters. The Dolans played card games, cribbage and euchre. We simply enjoyed each other's company; things were just fine.

And then we were invited to a friend's cottage for dinner. Friends of the family, retired publishers of the local newspaper in that part of Northern Michigan. What a lovely cottage, a stone fireplace, a large-screen television.

A second-floor master bedroom overlooked the lake, and they had their own private sandy beach. They showed concern about our primitive accommodations, namely our wooden shack. "If only we had advance notice you could have rented our daughter's cottage which is very similar to this place."

So kind, so well intentioned... but in the space of twenty minutes our hunger had returned with a vengeance! A hunger for the creature comforts of life that we thought we could do without.

As I write this homily, our son Dave and I are sitting in a fishing boat, miles out on the Lake Superior. I might add that so far we have not caught a single fish. A storm is approaching; black clouds and lightning fill the horizon. We need to pull up the anchor and head for the dock. We are both hungry!!

Our situation reminds me of Jesus in another boat on another lake, two thousand years ago. It reminds me of Jesus' teachings of the really important things in life. What true hunger is! And how it is satisfied: by a full and satisfying relationship with God through our Lord Jesus Christ.

Jesus Christ who says to us, *"I am the Bread of Life; whoever comes to me will never be hungry and whoever believes in me will never be thirsty."*

It is the last day of our visit to Northern Michigan. I am more acutely aware of what Jesus is saying to us: for us to maintain the right perspective in life; to hunger after the really important things, of real life, of truth and love and how to satisfy that hunger by a deeper relationship with our Lord.

Living within the boundary of God's love and protection

Jesus said, "Very truly, I tell you, anyone who does not enter the sheepfold by the gate but climbs in by another way is a thief and a bandit." Jesus goes on to say, "I tell you I, Jesus, am the gate for the sheep...whoever enters by me will be saved."

This Fourth Sunday of Easter is known to us as Good Shepherd Sunday; and in all three years of our Revised Common Lectionary we read the Good Shepherd monologue from the tenth chapter of John. This monologue is seen by some as a complicated passage, in that Jesus identifies himself as having multiple roles. He describes himself as the Good Shepherd, as the Gatekeeper, and as I have used as my text today, even as the Gate to the sheep-fold. Not only that, I have heard that this passage is defined as "theological, Christological, soteriological, eschatological, ecclesiological and ethical."

We are very much aware of commentators that always focus on the complexities of scripture rather than highlighting the simple and straightforward Christian message of love and caring for all peoples; the Good News of the risen Christ our Lord and Savior. Some of you are already aware that I subscribe less than one cent to these commentators' complexities; in fact I find them to be a distraction from our principal Christian mission in the world.

In Deacons' school, we studied for what seemed an interminable time some twenty of the most prominent Christian philosophers in history. We were given a question in our final canonical exams, "Who was our favorite philosopher… and why?" My answer was, I had no favorite because not one of them had any influence whatsoever on our Nicene Creed. I don't often comment on my results from that exam. Just let it be said I received a very high mark on my answer to that question. I thought at the time, boy, am I in the right Church and am I in the right Diocese!!!

From that preamble it is hardly a surprise that in this homily I would like to focus on a single aspect of today's Gospel: that our Lord Jesus Christ is the gate between our experiences in this world and the righteousness that is the lifeblood for our souls. What I mean by that is that our faith in the risen Jesus Christ means that in our day to day lives we always have access to Him who helps us decide what is the right thing to do when faced with temptation and the powers of evil. When our Lord Jesus is the gate between the world and our soul, then through the power and mystery of prayer He is always there for us. He will always help us differentiate between the thieves and the bandits, and those who really love and care for us and other people in this life.

Much of my working life here in the US has involved me in healthcare administration. Healthcare has grown to be the largest industry in this country. It is said that Ford Motor Company spends more dollars on healthcare than they spend on steel and now plastics for their automobiles. However as healthcare has grown per capita there has been a similar growth in get rich quick exploiters, embezzlers and other criminals in the healthcare business. My perception is that as the money has grown, so have the thieves and bandits, and so has the temptation to cheat the system.

In today's Gospel, Jesus talks about the sheep knowing the voice of the true shepherd. The sheep follow him because they know his voice. *"The thief comes only to steal and kill and destroy; I (Jesus) came that they may have life and have it abundantly."*

In the late 1980s I was the Administrator of a large, well known Medical Group in Chicago. A physician member of our Board of Directors invited me out to dinner to meet a business acquaintance of his. The setting was a storefront Italian restaurant on the west side of the city. There were some twenty tables with the famous red and white checked table cloths, and pictures of Italy on the walls. My associate, the physician, was already at the restaurant and he was arranging the tables in a particular manner with me to be seated at the head table.

Right on time the gentleman I was to meet, arrived, together with what seemed like an entire entourage. I was introduced to this "Jimmy Reeves" (rather an unusual name for a gentleman with such a strong Italian accent). The alarm bells had already started to ring in my head before we even started to consume a lavish meal with expensive wines. Was this a scene from the godfather or was it real? What was going on here?

In today's Gospel, Jesus is telling us, his flock, to be on our guard for temptation and false witness. When we hear a stranger's voice leading us in a direction we are uncertain about, then rely on our Lord the true gate for guidance…and we will be saved.

Back in the Italian restaurant, Mr. Reeves asked me about my job and the medical group, and he revealed that he owned and controlled two hospitals in Chicago. He then brought my associate, the physician, into the discussion indicating that the good doctor had been very helpful to him (Jimmy Reeves) over the years and that he, the physician, had been very well looked after. He then asked me what things did I enjoy in life… Travel? Booze? Cars? Women? Cuban Cigars? … on and on.

At that point in time my legs started shaking uncontrollably and I knew where we were going in the discussion. I am not ashamed in admitting I was scared to death. All I could do was to silently pray to God that I would not give in to this man, but that also I would leave that restaurant as healthy as when I walked in.

Jesus knew all about these types of situations. He himself had been tempted by the devil. He knew how the evil one presents himself to us in so many disguises. Our Lord knew only too well that all of us to a greater or lesser extent will, in our lives, be tempted to the evil side, whether it is as simple as exaggerating a deduction on our tax return or our expense reimbursement form at the office. Jesus tells us in today's gospel that when we hear a stranger's voice… that if we are ever tempted in this way… for us to look to him as the gate.

Jesus Christ is the only voice that we can truly rely on to make right decisions, decisions that will lead us down the right path, the path that leads us to God's Kingdom, to life eternal, in the arms of a loving and devoted God.

Jimmy Reeves turned up the heat. "John," he said, "I need more patient referrals from your medical group to my hospitals. I am told you are in the position to be helpful to me and I can see you are a sensible young man… I could tell right away we will have a highly profitable future together. My lawyer here is all ready to draft an agreement between us."

I held on to the table, and in the strongest voice I could muster said, "Mr. Reeves, I think there has been some form of misunderstanding here… and I am not available for this kind of agreement." I then stood up walked out of the restaurant and drove away.

There have been times when I have felt the presence of an Angel in my life. Maybe that was one of those times.

The risen Christ is with us Emmanuel… to help us make the good decisions, to help us resist temptation. To turn back the powers of greed and avarice in this world. To recognize and defeat the thieves and bandits in this life.

I would like to add a postscript to this story. About a year after the meeting in the restaurant it became clear that the physician member of the Medical Group Board of Directors had had a serious drug addiction for a number of years. Dr Brown's addiction was supported by his relationship with Jimmy Reeves.

Dr. Brown apparently committed suicide one year after his invitation to me to attend that dinner on the west side of Chicago. Let us pray for the soul of the late Dr. Brown, for Jimmy Reeves and all others who fail to hear the voice of Jesus the Good Shepherd… Jesus, the gate that leads to salvation.

Transformation into true believers

"They were saying, 'Is not this Jesus, the son of Joseph, whose father and mother we know?' How can he now say, 'I have come down from heaven?'"

Last Sunday was the feast of the Transfiguration. I regard this Sunday in many ways as Transformation Sunday: the transformation of us human beings into true believers that Jesus is the bread that came down from heaven.

All of us here today have concerns in our lives. To one extent or another we are concerned about our own welfare and position in this life, worried about making financial ends meet, concerned about our health and retirement, concerned with the needs of our kids and other loved ones.

Concerned with making our marriages and relationships work. Concerned with the disastrous compelling effect of drugs, alcohol and other addictions. Concerned about man's ongoing inhumanity to man, the seemingly endless bloodshed in the Middle East. The "have's" and the "have nots". Concerned with ideologies and priorities different from our own.

Our deep concerns when we are convinced we know the ultimate truth, because the Bible tells us in black and white. Then why can't I convince my neighbor that I know the truth and he doesn't get it? Concerns with how I stack up against my neighbor with his brand new Mercedes. Concerns with anger and jealousy while judging and stereo-typing the young well-dressed woman on the cell phone while she is driving a gas-guzzling SUV as large as an army tank. Concerns with the impact of change in our lives. Our rector, our leader, is leaving; what am I going to do? Who will I go to in time of trouble? Who will I blame when I am not happy with an issue at church or how I have been treated?

There is only one answer to all these human concerns. Without any doubt whatsoever in my mind, the answer lies in Jesus Christ our Lord and Savior.

Faith and love in Jesus completely and totally transforms our lives.

Through God's good grace we see the world in a different perspective, and we find ourselves able to turn over all our concerns to Jesus.

When we turn ourselves over to the Lord, then even in

Nazareth; Llandaff, Wales; Cissna Park, Illinois; the South Side of Chicago; whatever the town where we grew up, even in our home town they will recognize the transformation in each of us.

Those who knew us merely as the son of Joseph, the carpenter and Mary, or Walter the electrical engineer and Joan, or Carl the farmer and Dorothy; those who knew us as children growing up will see the transformation, the transformation into people who have come to know and love Jesus. People who understand that it is Jesus Christ, the Bread from Heaven who is the answer, the only answer to all our earthly struggles.

I first met Father David and his gracious wife Sally at their home in St Paul, Minnesota in November, 1986. I was senior warden of Emmanuel Episcopal Church, La Grange, Illinois, and I and the Junior Warden were meeting with the Rector-elect to work out the details of David's call.

Father David and I journeyed together along the same road for twenty years at Emmanuel, and I was asked the other day what was the one memory that stood out for me during this time.

In 1991 I was CEO of a very large physician medical group in Chicago. It was a tough job and my health was suffering. In the midst of that stress and chaos in my life, Father David asked me if I had ever considered ordained ministry in my life. That first question posed by David ultimately led to my being ordained a Deacon in February, 1996, and more importantly gradually transformed my life.

I am told by those far wiser than I that the transformation has nothing to do with dressing up in collars and fancy clothes. It is all about reaching out to others; to recognize that God is my boss... that all we do is for Jesus Christ; none of it is for ourselves. Through partaking of the Bread that comes down from heaven, then, but only then, can we help others with their earthly problems, and thus help ourselves cope with our own needs.

We have learned that John's Gospel, unlike Matthew, Mark and Luke, does not intend to present a chronology of historic events. John's Gospel, rather, is intended as a bigger picture analysis of the nature of Jesus the person and Jesus Christ the divine. In theological terms we call such a study Christology. John's Gospel from the outset was probably written for a much broader worldly audience than the Synoptic Gospels. John's Gospel has no stories of Jesus' birth or early life. We are plunged straight into Christ's teachings mostly written in an ancient style seen much in Old Testament writings and elsewhere, the style of using parables.

In that style and context, today we hear Jesus using a most familiar story from Jewish tradition. Manna, from the Egyptian word mennu for food, has a correlation with the Hebrew word for bread, manna, the bread from heaven that saved the Israelites in the desert from likely starvation. Jesus frequently uses parallels in his teachings. For the most part he uses them in a subtle form, but even when subtle, their meaning and effect is total transformation. The new Kingdom is at hand. He, Jesus from Nazareth, is the Savior, the Messiah, the Son of God. He, Jesus, is the true manna from Heaven, even in his home town of Nazareth.

In 1991 I told my mom in Wales that her son John was in the discernment process toward ordained ministry. Well, within 24 hours probably, the whole Parish of Llandaff were aware of this great change that was about to occur to her son. A certain long-time drinking buddy of mine heard the news in the local Post Office. It is purported that my friend's immediate reaction, after a lengthy period of uncontrolled laughter, was one of disbelief. "Dolan to wear a collar…you must be kidding! The only time I will ever see Dolan in a clerical collar will be holding a pint of beer at a costume party at the Black Lion." It would appear that my reputation as a young man was much more in the social arena than in the spiritual one.

It is said that when someone asked my friend Nigel whether it was true that Dolan the Chartered Accountant, the businessman, was going to become a "man of the cloth", the answer Nigel gave was that the rumor was in fact true; that Dolan was giving up business and accounting to become a tailor.

Jesus from Nazareth would never gain credibility in Nazareth in 30 AD just based on what he taught and proclaimed; and Jesus, it would appear, did not spend long enough in Nazareth in his adult years for the citizens of Nazareth to experience his transformation.

John as the ordained person would never gain credibility in Llandaff, Wales or La Grange based on just walking around in a clerical collar and trying to look holy. And as for David, the newly elected Rector of Emmanuel, it was his good deeds and caring for so many in our community that gave him credibility and evidenced his commitment to Jesus Christ.

Christians can only achieve credibility and demonstrate their transformation through their Christian action in the world. In their humility and love and caring for all people Christians must constantly demonstrate in their lives what Jesus taught us. Jesus said, *"Everyone who has learned from the Father comes to me."* If we have faith, if we live godly and repentant lives, that is all well and good. But if we demonstrate our faith in our actions toward others, then to use a common euphemism, we Christians "will have put our money where our mouth is."

If we reach out and love and care for each other the way Christ taught us, then, only then will even the people of our home towns, people from Nazareth; Llandaff; La Grange; Cissna Park, Illinois or the South Side of Chicago, wherever our homes of origin were, all will see a transformation and understand that we now live our lives differently, simply because we know, love and follow Jesus Christ.

Jesus Christ is the answer to the litany of worldly concerns that we all face at some time in our lives. Thank you Lord Jesus for our transformation into Christians.

No one except Jesus Christ has all the answers

From St. Paul's first letter to the Church in Corinth: "To each is given the manifestation of the Spirit for the common good."

What an inspiring set of readings we heard this morning! First, we hear Isaiah declaring that God rejoices over us: *"You shall be a crown of beauty in the hand of the Lord."* Then in the Epistle, St. Paul tells us that there are many kinds of people- because God the Holy Spirit wanted it that way, for his own purposes. And then, in the Gospel reading, St. John tells the wonder-filled story about how Jesus did something unheard of: he changed water into wine. And his disciples became believers.

When John Dolan was in his late twenties, the time of his

move from London to Chicago, professionally John had been told by many people that the world was his oyster. He had earned his ticket. "Go show those Yankee colonialists what you are made of!" It may come as no surprise to some of you that John was highly competitive; he was well educated with a Professional Degree, a British Chartered Accountant, equivalent to a CPA certificate. He had worked for ten years for one of the top public accounting firms in the City of London.

And then, when he joined Blue Cross Health Insurance Company in Chicago, in one year, in record time I think, John was promoted to Manager level and was responsible for teams of auditors working in seven states. He flew everywhere first class and attendant with that he became a first class eater, drinker and spender.

In his professional life John didn't aspire just to be knowledgeable of all the Medicare reimbursement issues he encountered. He felt he was the principal expert in his field and it was his responsibility to know all and everything there was to know about the world according to Medicare. He also went on to manage a clerical staff of nearly three hundred people at twenty eight years old.

And so on and so on; you get the picture. But in fact I find it difficult to write anymore because I am really beginning to make myself feel quite nauseous.

In Corinthians, Paul recognizes the variety of gifts that

God bestows on His people. Paul begins to discuss the human family working as a team in the world, all of us with unique gifts, dependant on God but also dependant on each other and on the gifts given through the Holy Spirit in our lives.

One day, Frank, my boss at Blue Cross, called me in for my regular evaluation. I knew what I was going to spend my raise on before I even went into his office. I had done a terrific job; all my contracts around the country had been completed and they were all under budget; I was certain that people liked me and appreciated my work. I was looking forward to this performance review.

"John," Frank started, "you and I both know the achievements you have made over the past year. You have done very well, but... do you have any idea what a pain in the neck you are to work with? Both for me as your boss and for those who work for you?" I was dumbfounded... what more could I have done?

Frank must have seen the horror on my face... but nevertheless he continued. "John, you must realize you are not the only talented person in the world. Could you perhaps allow me once in a while as your boss to come up with an idea or a thought that you haven't already thought of? Could you once in a while allow your staff to contribute from their wealth of knowledge and skills... even if you do know the answer yourself? John, you have done a good job; well done. But in the future, take a step back and allow others to contribute." Frank continued, "We are a large company. To succeed we need many diverse talented people. No one expects any of us to have all the answers all of the time. John, it is a good thing for you to say I don't know. It is a good thing to say, 'I need to check on that,' or 'I will refer to my colleague, to a Tom, Bill or Michael or Bob who may have a better handle on a particular issue.'"

St. Paul is saying that the early Christian movement in Corinth also needed all the skills available to them. No one person, however talented, could be the total answer. As the first major urban center to which Paul took his mission, Corinth needed sophisticated skills. Corinth was a major hub in East West trading; it was a complex, growing society. Thus Paul's advice to local leadership to recognize the diversity in skills available to them had to be key in the eventual successful development of the Church in that region.

John Dolan's personal journey encountered many future occasions when his own skills were not enough to solve the puzzles and challenges that life throws at us. His business life as an executive became manageable, not because his skills increased; but rather I began to recognize and value the skills of others. Also I began to understand that success depended on the correct combination of the huge variety of skills that God has given his people. But my journey did not really develop until I understood that all human beings are bestowed with God given gifts. It is simply a matter of how and if we use them. We all have gifts and we are all equal in God's love. I also began to recognize how generous God has been in his gifts to so many of us. As members of the community of deacons we are taught to listen and understand the value of all members of Christ's community. A large part of our job is to enable others to recognize their God-given gifts and talents to help them grow and flourish and thus benefit the whole Church. The deacon's job is not to step in and solve the world's problems, but rather to listen to others, to pray, and to encourage others to use their gifts to improve their lives and thus be able to help others.

St. Paul was successful in his mission to build the Church in large part because he understood the nature and benefit of God's gifts in others. He understood the power of the Holy Spirit present with us on our journey, introducing us to gifts in others that we might not recognize without God's presence.

I have encountered many wonderful, skilled people on my journey that have reinforced how generous and diverse our Lord is; and how recognizing all these different skills enriches our lives.

You may recall the story of my barber "Joe" and his ministry of listening to others. Of my former Spiritual Director who advises us to always look for God's gift even in the midst of what may seem a total catastrophe. Of Herman the "born again Christian" who bails me out of household projects when they go wrong, such as the project this weekend when the recently-installed shelves collapsed. And the most recent; Tom, my personal fitness trainer, who is attempting to help me turn the clock back, at least in some physical sense.

So at the end of all this, what have I learned traveling down this long road? I have learned that our Lord did not single me out and endow me with some set of super skills. I have learned to enjoy, and yes, employ the wonderful gifts of those around me; and that through those gifts I see the wonder and power of God's love.

But there is one more step on the journey: the "I's" and "me's" in the last paragraph are misworded. They should be "we's". I believe we as a community of faith are required and privileged by God to act as one, using all of our diverse skills to do God's work in the world. This is not an option for us. Whether it be in Sudan, Garfield Park or the city of Corinth, "to each of us is truly given the manifestation of the Spirit for the common good."

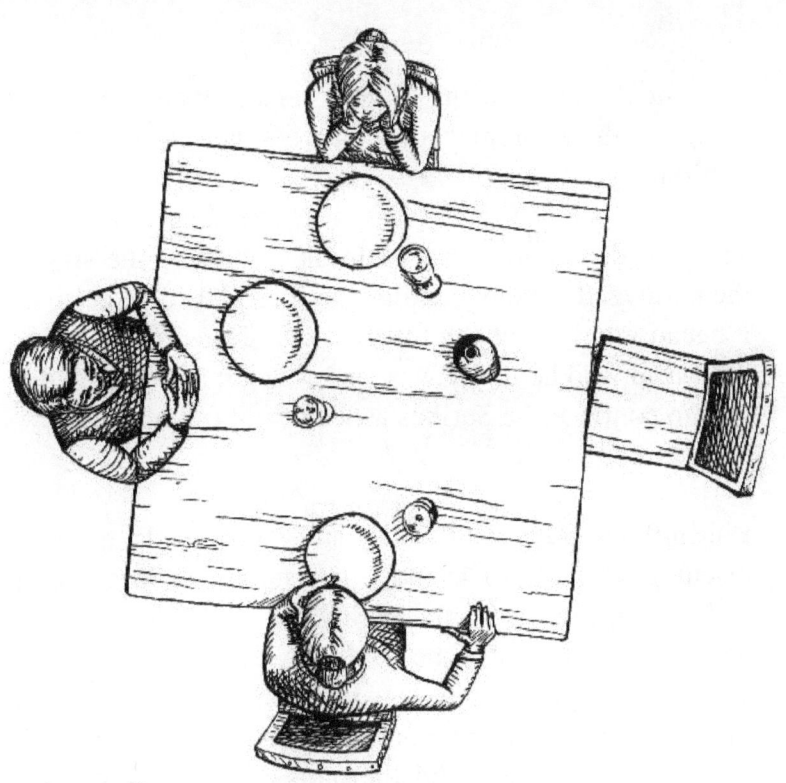

We are never alone...
Jesus Christ is always with us

"Then some people came, bringing to him a paralyzed man, carried by four of them..."

Most commentaries I have read, regarding today's gospel story, address the faith of the four friends and how their persistence in seeking Jesus resulted in the paralyzed man being healed. When faced with the crowds in and around the house where Jesus was speaking, the four men even removed the roof of the house so they could provide access for their friend to be healed by our Lord.

Commentaries go on to point out that not only was the paralyzed man healed of his physical disability, but that Jesus forgave the man his sins. Society believed that if a physical ailment came upon a person, then it was that person or their parents' sins that were the cause of the affliction.

There is also controversy in Jesus "forgiving the sins of the paralyzed person", and the scribes picked right up on it because only God can forgive sins. Jesus was showing the world who he really was, and was not reluctant in any way to confront the Scribes as leaders of established Jewish tradition.

But in the middle of this busy story, of crowds, of Jesus teaching, of faith, of friends' persistence, of forgiveness and healing, what did the paralyzed man feel? Did the paralyzed man want to be healed by this stranger Jesus? Did the paralyzed man want to be in the middle of the sawing, hammering, clamor and noise as the roof was being ripped off? How did the paralyzed man feel about being lowered by rope through a hole in the roof? Did the paralyzed man have any say on the matter or was he entirely at the mercy of those around him however well intentioned they were?

The paralyzed man may well have felt that in this precarious situation, balancing on a stretcher, held by just a couple of ropes, that once again he was a victim: he was exposed to danger, he was vulnerable, with no control on his life or his situation.

The paralyzed man must have felt very alone in this world. Alone, that is, until he touched the hand of God. Until he was healed by Jesus, the Son of Man, in that crowded house in Capernaum two thousand years ago.

My father, Walter Dolan, was a strong, intelligent man. Dad always appeared to have the answer to any problem;

and to me growing up he always seemed to be in control of situations. Many of you have heard my stories of his perceptive skills - the automobile, the mushrooms, the stolen seedlings. In our family he was always there. I never once saw him cry, and only a couple of times - and I will never forget those times - did he lose his temper. In our family there was a feeling that my dad was the rock.

Twenty-five years ago my dad suddenly became sick with a heart condition and, in the space of just a couple of months, we knew that he was going to die very soon.

I will never forget the feeling of isolation when I realized my dad would soon not be around anymore. Who would I go to for advice? Who would give me advice whether I wanted it or not? How could we survive as a family without Walter, my dad… the rock?

I felt vulnerable, isolated… alone. I had no control of whether or not my dad would die and my dad couldn't solve this problem. Maybe the paralyzed man felt that way. From the story today he certainly had no control on events as they unfolded.

In the late 1970s there was a rather bizarre and some say irreverent movie called "The Life of Brian". The British movie was made by The Monty Python guys, and in my opinion gave a unique perspective on many very familiar Bible stories. The following story owes a lot to the Life of Brian.

Brian is just an everyday sort of chap who is rather cynical about what he sees. In this adapted scene, Brian encounters the paralytic man soon after he was healed by Jesus.

Former-paralytic: Spare a talent for an old former-paralytic?
Brian: Did you say..."Former-paralytic"?
Former-paralytic: That's right, sir. Sixteen years begging, and proud of it, sir.
Brian: Well, what happened?
Former-paralytic: I was cured, sir.
Brian: Cured?
Former-paralytic: Yes, sir. A miracle, sir. God bless you for asking.
Brian: Who cured you?
Former-paralytic: Jesus did, sir. I was minding my own business one day with these four roofer friends of mine. All of a sudden they tell me, "We're going to see this Jesus. He will cure you; after all it's our fault you got injured in the first place. This Jesus... he will fix you up."
I really had no say in the matter. One minute I'm a paralytic with a begging trade, next minute my livelihood's gone. Not so much as a by-your-leave! "You're cured, mate." Those darn do-gooders.
Brian: Well, why don't you go and tell him you want to be a paralytic again?
Former-paralytic: Ah, yeah. I could do that, sir. Yeah. Yeah, I could do that, I suppose. What I was thinking was, I was going to ask him if he could make me a bit lame in one leg during the middle of the week. You know, something beggable, but not paralytic; to be honest you know.. being paralyzed was really quite inconvenient.

Brian then gives the former paralytic a coin... to which the former paralytic responds sarcastically, "Thanks so very much; a full half a denarii? Half a denarii for my whole life story?"

Brian then says: "There's no pleasing some people."
And the former-paralytic responds: "That's just what Jesus said, sir!"

It is very easy to feel isolated and alone in this life. Isolation distorts one's perspective of the world; it is hard to please or be pleased when you are out of step with the rest of the world. Immersed in anxiety, waiting for the results of a diagnostic test ... persons suffering from depression or severe physical disability. The isolation of feeling betrayed by those we trusted. The isolation resulting from personal financial problems or unemployment or dealing with chronic pain.

These are all situations where we can feel that life is out of our control. The feeling I experienced at age 38 when I realized my dad would no longer be around to be my rock.

All these lonely situations, all feelings of being out of control or lost, have but one solution; and that is the welcoming touch of the hand of God in the form of the love of Jesus Christ. We are never alone, not for one moment in this life. Jesus is with us loving us caring for us. Jesus shares in our pain and in our uncertainty and He tells us, "Do not be afraid or lonely. I am with you now and for always."

Jesus says, *"I am with you. I am all you need. My love will protect you and give you comfort. Just have faith in me and love me the way I love you."*

Jesus travels with us even in the fiercest of storms

"... He woke up and rebuked the wind and said to the sea, "Peace! Be still! Then the wind ceased, and there was a dead calm."

In today's Gospel, Jesus, tired from many hours of teaching to large crowds, left in a boat to journey to the other side of the Sea of Galilee.

I have been told many stories from visitors to the Holy Land about the Sea of Galilee. That early in the morning it is one of the most peaceful places on earth, to walk along the shoreline with the sun shining on the water and hearing the small waves lapping onto the beach... I am told it is a quiet place, a place for prayer and contemplation. A place where life is tranquil... It is one of those special places where we may feel closer to our Lord Jesus and the promises He made to us...

In 1995, I met Kathy Nagel. A quietly competent person, Kathy was an administrative assistant in my consulting business. Soon after I met her it became clear that this was a good time for Kathy in her life. She was now in a well paying job, a job that was difficult for her, but she was learning fast, with good prospects.

As a single parent, with no other living family, alone she had raised her son, Sean, now approaching his seventeenth birthday. It soon became very clear to me that Kathy knew very well that she was not alone on her journey... that Jesus Christ had been a trusted companion during good times and bad, and that Kathy had a loving Church family that was a safe place for her, where she was acutely aware of the presence of Jesus in those around her. Kathy's ironclad faith in our Lord Jesus Christ was very apparent, and we talked frequently about faith and the confidence it brings to us as Christians.

I am told there is a very different face to the Sea of Galilee from how it appears in the early morning. It is a face that Jesus and his companions experienced in today's Gospel. In addition to being a beautiful tranquil place, the Sea of Galilee was notorious for its storms... storms which would sweep down on travelers out of a clear blue sky, with little or no warning. The source of the storms were narrow ravines located on the eastern parts of the lake. As winds came off the mountains, the ravines act like wind tunnels, thus the storms encountered by Jesus and his companions were not unusual.

The sea was not a good place to be for travelers; besides the storms, travelers told stories of encountering ferocious sea monsters. Fact and fiction combine to create the level of fear we hear in today's Gospel...

The sudden, raging storm on the Sea of Galilee raised all the worst fears in the minds of the disciples, and their perception was that Jesus their teacher and master, wasn't with them, their Savior was asleep in the stern of the boat!

A raging storm hit Kathy Nagel in mid March of 1998. She had been experiencing some physical discomfort and went to the hospital for routine tests. On March 27th 1998, Kathy was diagnosed with terminal cancer of the liver. She was told that she would not see her son Sean's seventeenth birthday in September...

That same evening Kathy Nagel wrote me a letter. A letter to her boss, but also a letter to a Deacon, but most of all to a Christian companion. The letter was a positive celebration of her life on this earth; it was a "to do" list... of things that needed to be put in order... but above all it was a statement of faith and trust in our Lord Jesus.

Kathy had put herself completely in the hands of the Lord.

Her words were almost identical to those chosen by the late Cardinal Bernadin in his wonderful book, "The Gift of Peace." The day after the Cardinal learned that the cancer had spread to his liver and was inoperable, speaking at a communal healing service at St. Barbara Church in Brookfield, he said "We must believe that the Lord loves us, embraces us, never abandons us (especially in our most difficult moments). This is what gives us hope in the midst of life's suffering and chaos."

On the Sea of Galilee, in the midst of their storm, the disciples realized that Jesus was awake and with them... and with just a few words from our Lord, their storm became calm. But as with most of us, the disciples had to be reminded that God is with us, all the time. When the disciples recognized that our Lord was there in the boat with them all the time, then fearless peace entered their hearts.

For the remaining seven weeks of her life, Kathy Nagel was a shining example for all of us, of faith in our Lord Jesus Christ. She put herself completely in the hands of the Lord.

Jesus gives us peace always, even when life's problems threaten to engulf us in storms of tension, doubt and uncertainty.

Our Lord changes the darkness of death into the sunshine of life eternal. All of us faced with our own personal storms, whether it be sickness, sorrow, fear of danger or unemployment, we must all remember that God is with us, we can always put our total trust in Him.

Jesus is with us always. To voyage with Jesus is to travel in peace even in a raging storm.

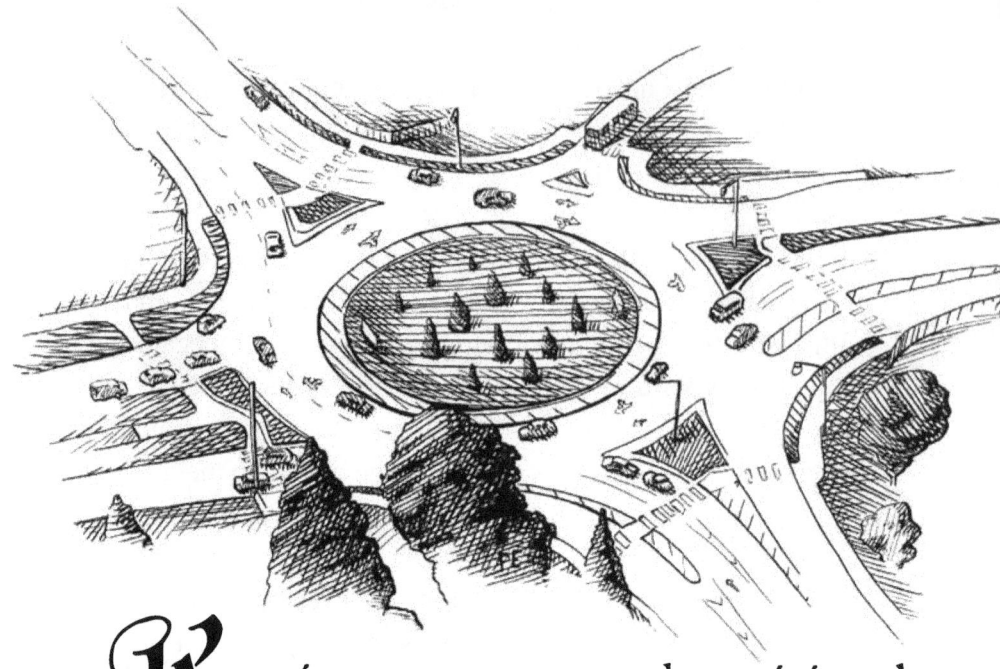

Keeping our eyes on the spiritual signposts in life

Many see today, Ash Wednesday, as a day of invitation. We are being invited to make certain choices, choices about being prepared for the future. We are being invited by God, through our Lord Jesus, to prepare ourselves for a more intimate relationship with our creator. We are invited into a period of preparation during which we can allow ourselves to be drawn in to the very heart of God. But we have to choose to go down the right road.

We live in a world where we are only too familiar with having to make choices. In fact we are faced with so many choices these days that it can be highly aggravating. In the food store just the other day, on one of the very rare occasions when I found myself shopping without the wisdom of my wife readily at hand, I found myself utterly perplexed. I wanted to buy just plain oatmeal, but I was faced with oatmeal with maple and brown sugar, oatmeal with apple and cinnamon, oatmeal with raisins, and all I wanted was plain OATMEAL.

If we make the right choice as to which road we follow as we enter this Holy Lent, we will need to work hard to avoid spiritual distraction. We are called to fasting and self-denial, in stark contrast to the hundred brands of oatmeal that we are pressed to buy, almost as if they were acts of patriotism. In a world where we are pressed to indulge ourselves in material acts of immediate gratification, we are called to spiritual planning and reflection.

In Great Britain where as many of you know, I grew up... well at least where I was raised... we don't have stop signs. Instead we are forced to deal with the monstrous invention called the "roundabout". In the US the roundabout is not unheard of; in fact in Massachusetts and parts of New Jersey they are known I believe as "rotaries". Why, there is even a rotary in neighboring Brookfield, Illinois!

But in the UK, the roundabout is what you face all the time; and I know there are forty-three roundabouts between Heathrow Airport and my sister's home just twenty miles away.

As with most things we face in life, when you drive on roundabouts all the time they are a piece of cake; but if you have never tried it or are an occasional visitor to the UK, the roundabout can be an absolute nightmare. The problems with roundabouts are threefold. Firstly, getting on them you frequently have to adjust your speed and make certain you avoid distractions. Secondly, when you are driving round the roundabout you need to know what lane to drive in to even have a reasonable shot at the third most difficult phase, how to get off the roundabout at the right road towards your destination.

As I prepared for today's homily, the image of Ash Wednesday and the planning and personal preparation for Lent seemed to me just like navigating a British roundabout.

Firstly, we have picked up quite a bit of speed as we have traveled through the Epiphany Season. Our Lord has been born into our midst, he has been revealed to us as the Son of God in Human form. We have perhaps developed a degree of comfort and ease that indeed Christ is with us Emmanuel.

Now things are changing: we must adjust our spiritual gears and be prepared for our Lord's last journey to Jerusalem. We must be ready to travel with him on that road. We have tools to help us adjust our spiritual gears: we have prayer, we have fasting, and we have the rites of transition. An important one of these rites is the Imposition of ashes this morning/evening.

The Imposition of ashes reminds us of WHO we are.

As the sign of the cross is traced on our heads, the first mark is in the shape of an "I". An "I" for someone who is uniquely me. "Me" the driver on my personal journey, with all my strengths and weaknesses, with all my God-given gifts and all my sins.

It also is the "I" that can be self-absorbing, distracting, separating us from the heart... from the Love of God.

It is said that the sign of the cross reminds us of WHOSE we are. The second, horizontal stroke of the ashes crosses out the "I" that leads to alienation from God. It is as if the horizontal stroke represents our being held in the outstretched arms of a loving Jesus. The horizontal stroke allows us to reach out to our brothers and sisters in community with Jesus Christ.

The sign of the cross reminds us to keep our attention on the road, to keep focused on Jesus' journey, to stay in the right lane on our personal spiritual roundabout.

The imposition of ashes helps us with another perspective on our journey. It reminds us of the context of the moment. The ashes are made from the palms of last year's Palm Sunday fronds. Thus the ashes point back to Jesus' journey.

I have read that the ashes are a reminder to us of the dusty roads that Christ traveled as he brought us the Good News of God's Kingdom. They remind us of again of a dusty road; but this time the dusty road Jesus will walk along when he reaches Jerusalem. It is the route that will ultimately lead to Christ's death on the cross for our redemption.

The third phase of our navigating the roundabout is for us to make sure that we are prepared for Jesus' journey to Jerusalem. We adjust our spiritual lives; we plan our personal programs of preparation through the various programs available to us.

We keep our eyes on the spiritual signpost by our maintaining an ever-closer relationship with God making certain that we travel in the right direction. This means putting competing self gratification on one side... and putting Christ first even closer than usual over the next forty days and nights.

I do not believe the season of Holy Lent means putting on garments of sackcloth and chastising ourselves; but I do believe this means spiritually examining ourselves, searching our hearts to make sure that we are practicing what we preach. Let us unclutter our lives and make the right choices. Let us reach out to each other and support each other as we travel this dusty road.

Let us pray that this period of Holy Lent prepares us, enlightens us, and keeps us well connected to the heart of our loving and caring God.

Be on red alert to challenges to our christian values

From the second chapter of St. Paul's letter to the church in Colossae: "See to it that no-one takes you captive through philosophy and empty deceit according to human tradition and the basic principles of this world rather than on Christ."

I believe St. Paul had a very clear understanding how one's human ego is stroked by achieving positions in society that offer power and influence over others. When he was Saul of Tarsus, prior to his dramatic conversion on the road to Damascus, Paul was a principal persecutor of Christians; and some scholars believe he was handsomely rewarded by the Jewish authorities for his terrorizing of the Christians.

Paul soon learned that devoting his life to our Lord Jesus

meant escaping the captivity of self aggrandizement and egoism. His material wealth and influence for evil was stripped from him. He now has one goal: to live at the foot of the cross that bears Jesus Christ. To put Christ first in all things, no matter how seductive the trappings of the material world may appear.

My wife Karen and I have recently returned from a vacation trip to Europe that inevitably included a few days in my beloved Wales. On occasion I have alluded to the rainy weather in Wales. Well, this year it has rained every day for the past four months. Welshmen themselves say there are two ways one can tell whether it is January or July in Wales. Firstly in January there are no leaves on the trees; secondly, in July the rain is slightly warmer than January.
In between frequent showers of rain, Karen and I visited Llandaff Rowing Club's Annual Regatta. This is a rowing competition involving various rowing clubs and universities. This is an event that I have not attended for forty years, but this Regatta was an event, which for me, was always close to heaven on earth.

In today's Epistle, Paul describes what for many of us is an ongoing challenge. The attraction of the new automobile... going into debt for the sake of being seen in a shiny new vehicle. Accepting a new client or job for the sake of the money... when one is aware of their dubious business practices. Failure to hold the line when faced with marginal ethical compromises, particularly in business. Membership in any human institution which seeks to exclude others because of gender, race, religious beliefs, sexual orientation, place of academic schooling or any other trumped up excuse that makes the members of the institution feel superior to other human beings.

I believe these are the types of philosophies that Paul is talking about in today's reading; but we have to be careful to discern and understand opportunities that flatter us, and we need to understand opportunities that appeal to our less desirable instincts, opportunities that may challenge our ability to always put Jesus Christ first in our lives.

When I was growing up in Wales, in my late teens the Llandaff Rowing Club became very important to me. Sure, I learned the techniques of rowing, but it was also an important focus for a social life. Rowing, much like club life in general, was an exclusively male domain in the sixties. There were also growing levels of social acceptance once you were accepted as a club member. I will never forget the day I won my first Regatta trophy... and immediately the older, more senior members of the club seemed to pay more attention to the young upstart, Dolan.

At the very top of the social ladder at the Llandaff Rowing Club was an organization called the Llandaff Waterman's Society. It still exists to this day: 30 men in a Society who only become members by personal invitation, and who are entitled to wear the most attractive and exclusive blue and gold necktie.

St. Paul as usual takes great care in the words he uses in his letters. *"Through philosophy and empty deceit"* is referring to the false distractions of Jewish and gentile teachers alike. The single word "philosophy" is a word used by the ancient scribes Philo and Josephus to describe the whole of the Mosaic Institutions. Pharisees and rabbis in general are seen by Paul as subversive to our faith in God through our Lord Jesus Christ.

In other words, in the modern idiom, we Christians are put on red alert. The world offers us all the sizzle we could ever want, but the real steak lies only in the values and teachings offered to us by our Jesus Christ. Only in Him can we come to fullness; He who is the head of every ruler and authority.

This was my second trip to Wales in 2008. The first trip in late May was to officiate at a friend, John Calder's funeral. At the funeral I met many of my Llandaff Rowing Club contemporaries, some of whom I had not seen since I was a teenager. This latest trip in July allowed me to reconnect again with many of the same people, people I rowed and socialized with as a young man. People I respected and who were an important part of my life.

At the Llandaff Regatta, in between the rain showers, Peter Johnson, an Officer on the Board of the Llandaff Rowing Club, approached me. "John," he said, "even though you live thousands of miles from us here at Llandaff, nonetheless you are seen to be a leader in our community. We have met as a Membership Committee and we invite you to be the newest member of the Llandaff Waterman's Society." He reminded me there are just thirty members and I am the youngest, but sometime in the next thirty years, should I still be alive, I will become President by rotation.

My reaction was one of total, absolute delight. As a young rower, I could never have imagined that I would be honored in such a way. I surely have reached the top rung of that particular social ladder in that corner of Wales. "Wow".
By that evening the euphoric dust began to settle. As many of you are aware I am surely blessed in that I am married to a most wise and thoughtful person.

As I described this Waterman's Society honor to Karen, she confirmed some discomfort that I already felt. How will your friends feel who live here and have not been invited to be members? How will your sister feel who has already been unable to share in your life at the Cathedral and elsewhere in the Welsh society? How does this Waterman's Society accommodate your diaconal ministry of availability and service to all human beings? Does the call of Jesus Christ fit into the "Waterman's" rather narrow view of equality in the world?

This past Thursday morning I shared Paul's letter to the Colossians and my concerns with a group of Christian associates; and a question was posed to me. Have you considered that God is the one really offering the invitation to this Waterman's group... so that you may bring influence to bear to reform the group... make it a more meaningful inclusive group... so that the group itself may be an instrument for Christ's work in the world?

I know the answer to that question.

Let us pray that we may always put Jesus Christ first in the world, and that so long as ethical behavior permits, that we Christians have the courage and will to work within existing institutions and organizations in the world to help redirect them according to Christ's needs.

The great high priest... or should I rather say our lord's humble servant?

In this brief reflection I would like to take the opportunity to thank God for bringing Karen, my wife, myself and our family to this place called Emmanuel Episcopal Church, La Grange, Illinois, exactly 27 years ago this past Ash Wednesday.

Also to thank God for bringing Father Tom Rosa, our Interim Rector, into our lives for this past 15 months from 2006 through 2007.

I remember the first couple of Sundays when Father Tom first arrived. I thought I was pretty versatile and experienced as a deacon working in the liturgy here at Emmanuel, but was I in for a rude awakening.

One moment we were seated in the middle, then on the left, then on the right. One moment there were two large candles on the altar. Then there were one hundred and two candles all over the place.

Good gracious! I knew it was an interim Rector's job to shake things up, but dear Lord, I felt so shaken up! I felt like one of Agent 007's vodka martinis, "shaken not stirred".

But then gradually I became stirred. I felt an awakening to the wonder and versatility of our Episcopal Liturgy, and I have loved every moment and I am very sad to see Father Tom leave us today.

Some of you have heard this story, maybe more than once, but I believe it deserves repeating.

The changes around here reached a crescendo, at least for me, at the midnight mass on Christmas 2007. Father Tom had laid out the vestments for the clergy prior to the service. The deacons were faced with wearing the most traditional gold and jewel encrusted dalmatics. For a simple soul like Deacon Dolan, I didn't know what to think… and what I did think was all about me; bad start.

I felt proud and maybe a little above other people. I felt overdressed and ridiculous. I felt, "Deacons are now recognized for who we really are." I felt, "What if Nigel and my buddies at the Black Lion in Wales ever see pictures of this? I will never live it down."

We lined up in the procession, and I was settling rather awkwardly and resigned into the role of assistant to the High Priest. And then my friend Tom Doyle came over to me, and he whispered in my ear. "Deacon John, you look like the ark of the covenant."

Bang! You could almost hear my ego balloon burst, and I laughed and enjoyed every moment of that service...and almost every moment of the past 15 months.

Working together with Tom Rosa, one of the most hard working, kind, self-effacing clergy I have ever had the pleasure to work with.

Bless you, Tom, for just being you and showing us the richness and diversity of our church.

With Father Tom as our guide through the wilderness this past 15 months, no wonder we have been able to call a Rector with the qualities of the Reverend Terri Stanford. No wonder we have achieved our Pledge Income goals. No wonder we have raised $20,000 for the clinic in Renk in Sudan... need I go on?

Tom Rosa, God bless you and thank you so very much for answering God's call to spend this time with us. Karen and I will always remember you.

Our place in the great universe

We heard this morning in Chapter 11 of the letter to the Hebrews: "Now faith is the assurance of things hoped for, the conviction of things not seen. Indeed by faith our ancestors received approval. By faith we understand that the worlds were prepared by the word of God, so that what is seen was made from things that are not visible."

Chapter 11 of the letter to the Hebrews is sometimes called Christianity's Hall (horl) of Faith. The chapter in fact serves as a roll call of many names familiar to even the most casual student of the Bible: Abel, Enoch, Noah, Abraham, Isaac, Jacob, Joseph, Moses among so many pillars of the Jewish tradition, all human beings who exhibited exemplary faithfulness to God, all worthy witnesses to our Creator.

But it is of course Jesus Christ who stands supremely among human beings as the "author and finisher of our faith."

Our conviction as Christians, our faith in life eternal, is not based on how well we emulate the great historic heroes of the past, but rather is based on what Jesus taught us, and his great sacrifice for us when he suffered so much, died on the cross, and then rose again so that we may be saved.

Some of you know this past month my wife Karen and I took a wonderful trip. We took our first-ever cruise, and it involved visiting among other places Italy, and the Greek Islands. There are not words to describe the sights and beauty of this journey, but one experience stands out for me.

Cruises generally have a variety of activities available when you are sailing the ocean blue, and on our trip, astronomy was one of the classes available. At midnight on the top deck of our 90,000-ton, twelve-storey-high cruise ship with all the deck lights extinguished, I experienced total darkness. For the first time in my life I saw the real night sky.

From horizon to horizon, north to south and east to west was a vast ocean of stars. Even our own Milky Way was visible like a ribbon or highway of stars winding its way across the sky, a sky containing billions of stars. The sight was totally, completely awesome, a sight that is now virtually unknown in North America, Europe or parts of the far East because of the growing effects of artificial light pollution.

Our friendly cruising astronomer/teacher, with his bright green laser pointer that seemed to reach the stars themselves, pointed out a particular constellation two thousand light years from earth. "Do you realize," he said, "that you are looking at an object as it was two thousand years ago, an object that was a witness to the time when Jesus Christ was alive?"

This vast blanket of stars is our universe, all the product of our creator God. I was overcome with the enormity of what I was seeing; and over the next few days it raised for me a number of important feelings and questions. I had a feeling of humility: that how much we human beings are privileged to be aware of our part in this enormous creation. I questioned how on earth we human beings can beat on each other so much when at the same time we are part of this vast universe, so much bigger than our petty differences.

When I looked up at the size of the universe, I felt so very small, which, by the way, is not a feeling that I experience very often (referring to my physical dimensions)! I felt like a grain of sand on a beach in the context of God's physical realm alone. How can I be of importance or be valuable to God?

I asked myself, what does this experience of viewing the enormity of God's physical creation do for my personal faith?

We will come back to these questions. But first back on earth, with our feet well planted in our faith in our Lord Jesus Christ. Not gazing at the heavens but with our eyes focused on the mystical nature of God's grace, what does the Letter to the Hebrews tell us about faith?

Jesus told us that faith is the certainty of God being Creator. Those of us who believe in God, simply and sincerely believe that He is the Creator. Then everything else makes sense and falls into place.

Faith is pleasing God. People of true faith demonstrate that faith by making every effort to please God before self. Faith is oriented to the future. In the modern world, material faith is very different. It has been stated that material faith is being certain that what has been promised will be provided, and with true faith there is a willingness to let everything else go, even life itself. The Greek word for faith is "pistis" – which also means faithfulness. True faith, faith in God, is at the heart of faithfulness. Without faith, faithfulness weakens; wariness takes over, resulting in the danger of one denying one's own faith.

And the answer to all the questions and concerns raised by my view of our Creator's universe? The answer to all concerns we have in this life is our Savior Jesus Christ. The stars in their millions or billions, even trillions, simply represent in themselves one by one, atom by atom a part of the "great cloud of witnesses" to faith in God through Jesus Christ.

I also came to the conclusion that each of us human beings is as important to God as any atom in the vast universe. What a wonderful feeling.

Providing safe places for each other

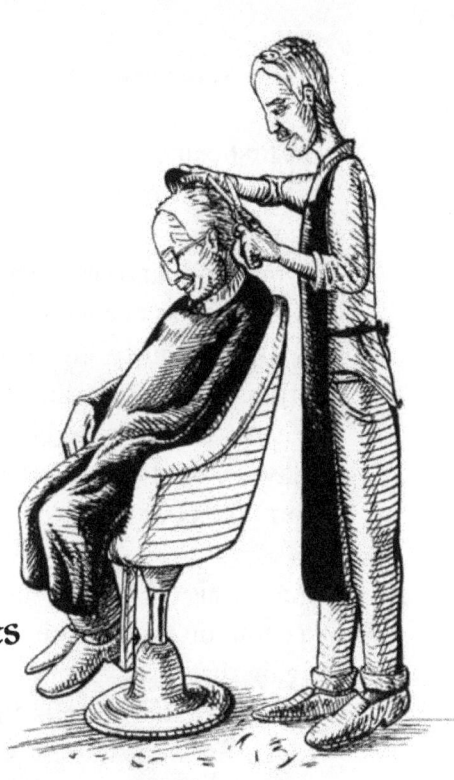

"So if I, your Lord and teacher, have washed your feet, you also ought to wash one another's feet."

Maundy Thursday – "Maundy" derived from the Latin mandatum meaning "commandment" and the Middle English "maunde," the ceremony of washing the feet of the poor on Maundy Thursday.

Maundy Thursday… "the stories of the night before." The night before the crucifixion of our Lord Jesus Christ, but also the night before Israel's flight from Egypt, the night before the Passover. It is the night when God prepares His people for events to come. It is the night when we need be prepared for the suffering and death of Jesus tomorrow.

We live in hope of the resurrection. Our experience tells us that it will come - but tonight we must remember and focus on being prepared for the most difficult part of our Christian journey, the death of our Lord Jesus.

In first century Palestine, the act of foot washing was not a ritual or act of religious consequence. Foot washing before the evening meal was a practical necessity. It was no more symbolic than our washing our hands before dinner. Foot washing was needed because feet shod in open sandals, feet walking in dusty streets, by the end of the day became pretty gross. The unpleasant and demeaning task of foot washing was an act performed by the lowest in the food chain - even slaves would argue among themselves as to who would perform the onerous task.

And Jesus once again turns the world upside down. He uses a common every day event in foot washing to illustrate once again that in His kingdom it is our humility, and our caring for each other, that is important. Strike the word important... it is our humility and caring for each other that is a requirement for us to be a follower of Jesus.

Once a year the Dolan family would travel from Wales to spend a week with my dad's mom in the south of England. Nana, my Grandmother was a formidable lady. She lived to 96 years of age and most everyone in the family was intimidated by her until the day she died. A week as a family staying with Nana was like walking on eggshells, or should I say a minefield. You never knew when you would be the one in the crosshairs to be the recipient of Nana's wrath.

As a child I thought it very interesting that my dad continually needed to go to the store, or leave the house when we were staying with Nana, whereas when we were home he would never leave the house. One of the places he would always go to was to the barbershop, sometimes twice in the week of our stay. He would go for a haircut even if he had had one just before we left Wales.

I went with Dad one time and discovered that the barber was a very old man, and my dad had been going to him since my dad was a boy. What I also remember about that old-fashioned barber's shop was that it was quiet there. That the barber and my dad talked a little, but in low voices, and I particularly remember my dad was smiling when he left that place.

In that Upper Room on the night before the greatest of ordeals, Jesus taught his disciples to follow his example. By Jesus' washing his disciples' feet he was displaying an act of the greatest humility, but he was also showing them how much he deeply loved and cared for them; and that is how he intended his disciples treat all people. Jesus said, *"So if I, your Lord and Teacher, wash your feet you also ought to wash one another's feet."*

For the past fifteen years I have gone to the same barber. Joe is the old-style men's barber. I don't go to see Joe to escape an unpleasant experience at home, but over the years I have developed an understanding of why my dad smiled when he left that barber's shop.

When I first would see Joe the barber, I was a young hotshot company executive. I would call ahead and explain how valuable my time was, and could he fit me in at a special time. Sitting in the chair I would impress Joe; particularly coming from the British Isles, and I would tell him about all my experiences.

But then over the years things started changing. I started listening and hearing about Joe's life and experiences, and I began to realize how important he is to many people, and how important his customers are to him. I understand why many regulars will wait forty-five minutes for Joe to cut their hair. People don't just wait for Joe because of his haircutting skills. They wait for his quiet respect for those sitting in his chair, his gentleness, his kindness, his humility, his ability to listen and remember the important things.

Recently Joe had two hip replacements and was gone for eight months. I missed him greatly, and when I saw him again I realized how important Joe is to me in my life and the value of that quiet time in the barber's chair. It represents a safe place in a hectic world, and God speaks through people like Joe the barber.

I now understand why my dad would go to a safe place, and have two haircuts in a week when he felt under attack at his mother's home.

I understand that Joe the barber washes my feet in exactly the way that Jesus teaches us tonight. And I have learned from Joe by responding to the kindness with similar feelings of caring and gratitude.

As we prepare ourselves for the events of Good Friday, let us each think about additional ways we can wash each other's feet. That extra word of encouragement, or expression of love and caring. That one less word of unnecessary criticism. The sensitivity to listen to Joe the barber's life and experiences and not fill the air with stories about ourselves and our achievements. Let each one of us provide a safe place for someone who is in need of a listening heart.

Let us love and care for one another in the same way that Jesus showed his love for us by giving up his life on the cross for our redemption.

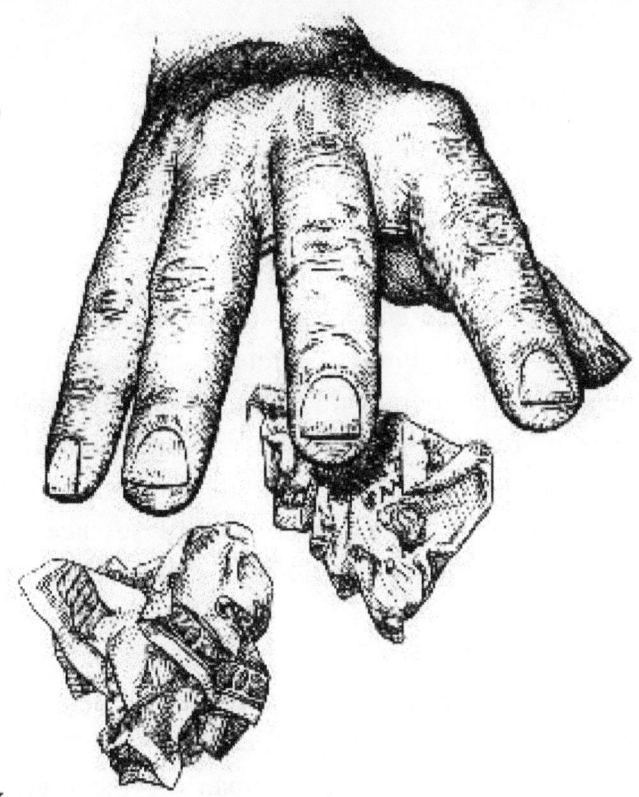

Following the courage of our convictions

"When they were satisfied, he told his disciples, 'Gather up the fragments left over, so that nothing may be lost.'"

In today's Gospel from the story of the feeding of the five thousand we hear two distinct messages.

We understand clearly that the food that our Lord distributes represents the love of God through his Son our Savior Jesus Christ... the spiritual food that we need and accept as the nourishment vital to be members of his kingdom.

The second message I hear is for the human race to act and behave as a single community... for us to share our God given abundance... so that we help each other... with the result that all people receive as much as they need.

As Christians, I believe we each need to address individually, how this sharing of God's bounty fits with the profit motives of a free enterprise society. How it fits with the rights of an individual to create as much wealth as he or she desires, as long as it's legal. How it fits with the vast range of political and religious perspectives around our tiny globe we call earth. How it fits with close to 40 million Americans with limited or no health insurance and facing personal bankruptcy should there be an onset of a catastrophic illness.

Jesus' whole attitude to the world is that he acts with the assumption of abundance rather than scarcity. He understands the hollowness of a human life pursuing material possessions, particularly money. In contrast he tells us over and over again that the love of God is endless... it will never be depleted, and will provide us every nourishment that we will ever need or want.

For many years my professional, business life has been as a financial consultant in the healthcare industry. It just happens that in recent years I have tended to be adviser to the higher monetary compensated, surgical specialists. This has produced a more than reasonable income contribution to our household.

About a year ago I was attending a client's regular board meeting. Normally the nine owners all attended the meeting... discussions were broad ranging and generally constructive. You might take note that two of the nine owners earned in excess of $1.5 million per year after malpractice insurance; the seven remaining owners earned an average of $600,000 per year.

At this particular Board meeting, neither of the two highest earners could be present. The remaining seven owners spent the entire meeting complaining about their meager level of compensation, and discussed how could they move more money to their accounts and improve their annual incomes of a mere $600,000... and they looked to their financial consultant Mr. Dolan to help them achieve this.

John's Gospel mentions that the Passover, the festival of the Jews, was near. It is believed this is not incidental information. It was deliberately included in the Gospel because it provides a reminder of Jewish history, specifically the slavery in Egypt under the heel of the Egyptian Pharaoh. The bread of Pharaoh was the bread of fear, scarcity, and slavery. Pharaoh demanded your very life and even still, there was never enough.

Thus Jesus' teachings of the abundance of the love of God was seen in stark contrast to Jewish history and experience.

The seven surgeons earning an average of $600,000 live with a similar view of the world as Jewish history. They see life from the perspective of fear, because each has taken on excessive financial obligations, to provide themselves and their families with very expensive standard of livings. Scarcity... because they did not recognize abundance... also evidenced by their hiring entry level office clerical staff at minimum wage.

These owners had become slaves to the lure of money.

The discussion at the board meeting was distasteful to me and I am sure would have been to everyone in this place here today. In fact the attitudes in the meeting made me feel physically nauseous...

I discussed the facts that evening with my wife and family... why am I using my skills and experience in such an environment. I soon after resigned from the consulting engagement... which incidentally reduced our household income by close to 60%.

We live in a world that is filled with inequities, corruption, greed and despair living alongside love, compassion, hope and righteousness. It is an ongoing battle. But the only answer to the problems we face is to follow the teachings of our Lord Jesus Christ. To let the love of God rush in and fill our hearts and replace the negative feelings and human cravings that, if we pursue, just make us feel even more empty.

How do we reconcile today's Gospel with a world where, in the same week we hear of alleged defiling of graves to sell the same lot twice or more times to unsuspecting customers. We then hear of a well known investment bank, which in six months has recovered from the brink of disaster to making record profits in the second quarter of this year, and then quite legally paying massive bonuses to its employees. As the Financial Times described it this week, the yachts are again being purchased by the bank employees, not the customers nor the shareholders, other than a certain well known investor... who invested at the riskiest time and has made $3 billion profit.

I believe one answer is that we in the church need to do a

better job of harvesting the gifts that are available within our society, so that we become more able to provide for the most needy and most vulnerable among us.

A former Suffragan Bishop of Chicago, once told our assembly of Deacons a story about the feeding of the five thousand and how Jesus was able to feed so many people from such limited resource.

The Bishop indicated that many of the crowd gathered on the mountain would have been shepherds… and it was customary for shepherds to carry a lunch of a dried fish and bread. The food was usually carried in a leather pouch attached to a girdle tied around their waist. The food was also hidden under their cloaks to keep it away from the heat of the sun.

When the shepherds were invited to sit down, to listen to our Lord, the act of sitting down opened their cloaks and exposed the food they carried with them. Thus a huge amount of additional food was available, which, combined with the five barley loaves and two fish provided more than enough food for all those present.

Our Lord Jesus is the full and only answer to concerns about scarcity and vulnerability, that we all face in our lives.

If we put our complete faith in God and act and behave as a single community, then our Lord will provide for all and every need we will ever have.

The power of prayer and hope for new beginnings

From the Book of the Prophet Isaiah: "A voice cries out in the wilderness prepare the way of the Lord, make straight in the desert a highway for our God. Every valley shall be lifted up, and every mountain and hill be made low; the uneven ground shall become level, and the rough places a plain. Then the glory of the Lord shall be revealed, and all people shall see it together, for the mouth of the Lord has spoken."

For a number of years, early on a Friday morning a small group of my clients and friends have met for breakfast to talk about Jesus Christ's presence in our daily lives. We are a diverse group: a health care administrator, an African American originally from Nigeria, an officer of a local bank, two sales folks, and me. It is a very focused group, and we pray together. We have shared with each other that we all feel spiritually uplifted and strengthened when we are together, and we regard the group as a great gift from God.

The readings for this day, the second Sunday of Advent, are all about hope, hope as a community for a new beginning. In the Book of Isaiah it is about a new Exodus, the consolation of the people of Israel and the expectation of their return from exile in Babylon.

In Mark's Gospel we have a direct link to Isaiah, again hope for a new beginning for God's community. Hope of radical change from the domination of both the high priestly rulers within the Jewish community and their imperial Roman overlords.

This past Friday, our group met as usual at our table in the far corner of the restaurant. Toward the end of our discussion, a young woman who had been sitting two or three tables away came over to us. She was in a distraught emotional state with tears pouring down her face. She said four simple words to us: "Do you gentlemen pray?"

We said we do, and we asked her to join us. She said something dreadful had happened to her, and she was not able to even speak about the details, but asked if we would pray for her. We said we would.

With that the stranger left the restaurant, and we saw her drive away.

One knows when something is real; this was real. When she initially approached our table, our suspicions were raised that she was looking for a handout in some way.

But this was different. We prayed together for this young woman and whatever her needs may be. We prayed that she might experience hope in her life, and that the traumatic event, whatever it be, be replaced with a new beginning.

We were all left feeling shell-shocked. What courage it must have taken to approach this diverse group of strangers!

In this particular season of Advent we are continually being bombarded with bad news about the economy. It is almost as if the worse the news gets, the more the presenters rub their hands together with delight. The worse the news the better, the more the blame, the more scary the prognostications for the future... the more advertising revenue increases and the more newspapers are sold.

In Advent, this season of Christian Hope and preparation, I feel a sense of sorrow for those that wallow in the misery to profit themselves, but in so doing cause worry and angst to many millions of people on Main Street. We pray this also changes in the coming of Christ's kingdom.

Much of the Book of Isaiah is like watching CNN or listening to Bill O'Reilly on Fox: countless chapters of doom and gloom. Whether it be Assyria, Egypt, Babylonia or Ethiopia, international partners could not be trusted. Israel was on its own, with little or no chance of breaking the bonds of slavery. But today's reading from Chapter 40 is radically different: there is a realization of hope and faith that there will be a better tomorrow.

Back at our small gathering on Friday, we were all affected emotionally by this young woman's brief presence in our lives, and the great privilege of praying to our Lord for the angels to hold her, and God's blessings to heap down on her and relieve her distress.

A few minutes later, the owner of the restaurant came to our table. He said that he had just received a cell phone call from a young woman that had been in the restaurant earlier that morning. She asked the owner if he would pass a message to a group of gentlemen sitting together at the back of the room.

The message was that she had just heard that the great problem in her life had been miraculously resolved. The four of us just held hands and tears ran down our faces. A stoic Norwegian banker, a tough much travelled sales executive... all of us... were stunned by what had happened. But we were left with the sense of the power of hope, of prayer and faith.

Anything is possible in this life through the power of faith in our Lord Jesus Christ.

Opening our hearts to reveal the glory and love of God to others

From St. Luke's Gospel: "And while Jesus was praying, the appearance of his face changed and his clothes became dazzling white."

Today is the Feast of the Transfiguration. The word "transfiguration" is defined in our dictionaries as "a change in form or appearance", "an exalting, glorifying or spiritual change."

Today's lessons describe the glory of God revealed to humankind in a very real and powerful way. They also describe the resulting transformation from two experiences: Jesus appeared in dazzling white, transfigured or revealed as the Son of God, but his appearance also had a profound transforming effect on the human witnesses who were exposed to the power and glory and love of God.

Today's story is one of the rare times in the Bible where the tremendous glory of God is revealed directly to human beings. Most of the time we read of God's glory as revealed in more subtle ways, such as through miracles or wise teaching. Today's text from Luke involves God's glory directly revealed by Jesus.

Many, if not all of us, have had experiences in our lives when God's glory and his love are revealed to us through the special acts of others. When these situations arise it is my experience that these individuals "glow." They light up... they glow... both in a physical sense, but also in a sense of presence; they know their behavior is in communion with Jesus Christ. They have behaved in a way that, in their heart, they truly feel they have represented and revealed the love of God to the world.

Peter Evbuoma is a friend and former business client of mine. Peter is a black African from Nigeria, who is now part owner of a successful physical therapy provider network in Chicago. Peter was raised a Roman Catholic in Nigeria and immigrated to this country some twenty years ago. Some time along the road, Peter (in his words) says that the love and glory of Jesus was truly revealed to him. As a result of this, Peter has become a soldier for Jesus Christ. Peter experienced a spiritual transformation in his life that has resulted in his putting our Lord first in all phases of his life.

A few weeks ago Peter was in his favorite breakfast spot in Chicago. He is well known there, and has a favorite booth. The waitress welcomed him and started to prepare the table for him. At that moment another black guy arrived dressed in gang-related gear with tattoos, earrings and heavy boots, with an angry, menacing expression... you get the picture. This guy pushed ahead of Peter and took possession of the booth.

Peter momentarily backed off; a sense of fear briefly brushed past him. Then he decided he would slide in the booth opposite this aggressive-looking interloper. Peter ignored initial threats from this other guy, and he stayed at the table.

For the next twenty minutes or so, the angry guy harangued Peter about the "white" dominated society: that there was no hope for the black people other than fighting back. Then Peter said to the angry gang member, "Look, I don't know if you have noticed, but I am blacker than you; and I don't have any of the problems you describe." The guy asked Peter, "What's so special about you? What makes you different?"

Peter Evbuoma answered, "Life is different for me because I know and believe in Jesus Christ. The love and glory of God, through his son Jesus Christ, has been revealed to me, and this has changed my life."

The response from the supposed gang member was extraordinary. He listened quietly, he responded emotionally, and the end result was that Peter has had subsequent meetings with the gang member encouraging him to find a different path in his life, a path that hopefully one day soon will lead him to Jesus Christ.

I will never forget Peter's expression as he told us this story: his face glowed because he knew our Lord was also at that table with those two men at breakfast that morning.

On the mountain top two thousand years ago, Jesus revealed to his closest disciples the heavenly transformation to glory that awaits all the saints of Christ.

The transfiguration of Jesus Christ, the revealing to his closest disciples that he was the Son of God, appears to have had a profound effect on the three disciples Peter, James and John. Peter, hardly a man at a loss for words, was clearly astounded at the sight of Jesus in the company of Moses and Elijah. All Apostle Peter could muster was some mumbling about building a residence for these awesome beings.

Two years ago three of our leadership group at Emmanuel La Grange, attended a workshop at our Diocesan Convention concerning a mission to the people of the Diocese of Renk in Sudan. As a result of what we learned that day, a seed was planted at Emmanuel, with the hope and prayers that we could in some way make a difference for a people in Sudan, so poor that bark soup was considered a luxurious meal.

Since that time we at Emmanuel have become a partner parish to St John in Melut in the Anglican Diocese of Renk, Sudan. We pay many of the administrative expenses to support that Parish, and the mission has enriched many lives at Emmanuel.

Last week a certain Jean Owen in our community, announced to our congregation that our Board has agreed that we will raise the $16,000 necessary to allow St. John's Melut to build their first medical clinic. Also to hire one trained medical assistant to start the program. Jean Owen's face glowed as she described this project to us. "Who would have thought," she said,"that we could have made such a difference."

The love and glory of God has been revealed to Jean. She understands the transforming power of God's love at work in the world. Transforming for the people of Melut, yes, but perhaps even more transforming for Jean Owen and her committed team of missionaries.

The three disciples in Luke's Gospel today, were transformed in themselves at seeing direct evidence of the divine nature of Jesus. They experienced the total love of God for us human beings, manifested in the presence of God's only son Jesus Christ in the world.

I believe the opportunity to experience the transfiguration, the revealing of the glory and love of God, is all around us and available to us. Sometimes the opportunity is presented to us in the most unlikely of circumstances, such as Peter Evbuoma in that restaurant where his own life could have been in danger…. or in that creative workshop in the Church Convention, at a time when most of the Convention was distracted by negativity through division and dissent.

Let us give thanks to our Lord Jesus Christ for all the opportunities he provides for us to reveal to the world the glory and love of God.

God's gifts in the midst of chaos

Even before the full effects of the simmering world financial crisis hit the headlines, 2008 had already been a tough year for the Dolans, for my wife Karen and me. As one of my southern colleagues puts it, the year has been, "Oh Lordy, Lordy… what next?"

It all started in March right here at Emmanuel. Between services with my profuse nosebleeds, a symptom of sky high blood pressure. Profuse nosebleeds… indications that were the first sign of my dad's terminal heart condition back in the 1980s.

I was doomed.

The next experience was getting to know the ER better than I know the Black Lion Pub, in the village where I was raised in Wales. I was then obliged to encounter an endless stream of medications that had not been invented when my dad was sick all those years ago, but which provided me with every side-effect you can imagine. From fatigue that would cause me to fall asleep in business meetings, to fluid retention that made me look and feel like the Pillsbury Doughboy.

Then we had the cardiologist in his wisdom, putting his hand on my arm and saying, "John, you are a real challenge. Your condition is not life-threatening... but we are running out of options." The option I took was to change my cardiologist.

Then you may recall my wife Karen broke her arm, which resulted in months of frustration. Three months alone for my learning where the on/off switch for the washing machine was... oh, and learning how to push the cart at the food store.

And why on earth would she break her arm while I was going through all this heart stuff? Had she no sense of timing? Then I had to enroll in a cardiac rehab program; but only after Karen's rehab. Then the news of brother-in-law Bob's illness... and on and on.

To cap it all off, there was the episode in Church a month ago: I swooned and started to keel over, while reading the Word of God. I frightened my family and friends. What on earth is wrong with me to allow that to happen!!! What a story of misery and suffering...but at least we have limped and stumbled our way as far as Thanksgiving. But even now Karen has been sick at home with the flu for two weeks!

And now they are asking us to give thanks! Thanks for what? A couple of years ago in the United Kingdom, Queen Elizabeth described a particularly bad year for the Royals as their "Annus Horribilis". I now know what she meant.

I have asked myself in recent weeks, why me, why us? We are supposed to be the good guys. We tithe, we offer help to others both in our work and in our Community of Faith... why should we, the Dolans, be singled out to go through all this suffering? We should have life a lot easier than this.

Hmmmm. In the real world have you ever heard such a litany of self-serving, self pitying, utter nonsense? But I have to admit it was sort of fun describing our experience in that way; because if we are truthful we all share these feelings from time to time.

In today's Gospel story, one of the ten lepers, when he saw that he was healed, turned back, praising God with a loud voice. He prostrated himself at Jesus' feet and thanked him. But where were the other nine? Probably angry and upset that they had lost all those years of their lives. They had been forced to be isolated, away from their loved ones. What did they have to thank God for? He had betrayed them and allowed them to suffer. They had not deserved all the pain and being socially outcast.

The Gospel story sounds rather too familiar and too close to home for my comfort level!

Let us pause for a moment, and take a somewhat different view of this past year for the Dolans. Where are God's gifts in what we have experienced during this phase of our lives?

- We have experienced the love and prayers of our friends and family, especially our friends at Emmanuel
- Karen and I have experienced growing closer together in facing and dealing with adversity. (At least after I was able to work the washer and dryer!)
- We have experienced the wonders of the advancements in medicine.
- We have learned patience and a reprioritizing of commitments in our lives.

- I have experienced the bonding that occurs when a group of patients travel through a rehabilitation program together.
- To appreciate the commitment and professionalism of Melanie and Betsy, the Nurse and Trainer responsible for the program.
- We have learned how one hears God's voice in the quiet of the night, in the midst of worry, pain and discomfort.
- We have learned that even when we are faced with our own problems, we are still available to offer a hand to others in need.
- I have been particularly reminded of how much my dear spouse contributes to the smooth running of our home and our life together.
- We have been reminded that even in what may seem the most catastrophic events in our lives, God presents gifts to us in the midst of the chaos. Our challenge is to find and use those gifts.
- We are reminded that God loves us, particularly, I believe, in our vulnerable moments. We thank God from the bottom of our hearts for each other and for the gift of His Son our Savior Jesus Christ.

On this Eve of Thanksgiving day, "Let us truly give thanks to the Lord our God... It is right to give our thanks and praise."

Standing firm in one spirit with integrity

From St. Paul's letter to the Church in Philippi: "Live your life in a manner worthy of the Gospel of Christ, so that, whether I come and see you or am absent and hear about you, I will know that you are standing firm in one spirit, striving side by side with one mind for the faith of the Gospel, and are in no way intimidated by your opponents."

Firstly let us put this letter in context. Paul is writing the letter from prison, probably in Rome, and it is thought that he is awaiting trial. Paul is clearly uncertain about his future if he has one at all, at least in this life.

But in spite of this situation, Paul offers Christ and himself as examples of courage and self-surrender in the face of suffering and death. He urges the young church in Philippi to hold together in the face of opposition and temptation. He urges integrity to the Gospel of our Lord Jesus.

I cannot imagine a set of readings that we have heard today to be more appropriate for the financial times we are living through...particularly this past week.

Huge financial institutions, household names to many of us, have failed. Property foreclosures are commonplace, Wall Street is tottering and, God forbid, the Federal Government is attempting to pick up the pieces, pouring billions of taxpayer dollars into the private sector.

A friend of mine in England, like many of us not particularly well versed in the intricacies of global finances, called me the other day and said, "I know what's caused all this mess! It is those two Americans, Fanny and Freddie that are the cause of all the trouble."

Paul's letter to the Philippians is all about maintaining personal integrity. Paul is telling us to hold fast to the examples laid down by our Lord Jesus Christ and not be tempted by other influences in this life.

In my opinion the first contribution to the financial woes the world is facing is pure and simple greed. Giving in to the temptation of excessive wealth, particularly acquiring wealth where there is little or no physical work involved.

The second contributing factor is putting self before any community responsibility. Again it is right here in today's readings. For CEOs of major financial institutions to be paid millions of dollars in compensation based on the number of loans the institution has made, while the company itself is heading toward bankruptcy, is hardly as St Paul put it *"striving side by side with one mind for the faith of the Gospel."*

Despite the misfortune of those who worked for him, Lehman Brothers Chairman Richard Fuld, at the time of writing, still had his $10 million mansion in Greenwich, CT, as well as an oceanfront estate in Florida and a luxury Park Avenue co-op.

I read a letter to a London Newspaper this past week. The writer said that he had felt a great deal of sympathy, particularly for the executives of financial institutions who had been laid off. They had spent all those years building the businesses and now it was all gone. But something happened this past week that totally changed the writer's mind.

During his lunch break, the writer was walking past the office of Lehman Brothers, and he saw a very well dressed individual leaving the office with a box in his arms, which clearly contained his personal effects. But then he took a closer look. The box was an empty case of expensive champagne!

The setting in Matthew's Gospel today is also becoming more and more familiar to us in modern times: the fear of being unemployed or under employed, the fear of earning enough money to put bread on the table.

The story of the vineyard describes extraordinary generosity, but it also highlights the truth that God provides the needs for all of us, not just the privileged few. Some describe this as the "manna truth," a reminder that in the Book of Exodus, God provided for his people with manna from heaven, that saved them from starvation.

The owner of the vineyard was similarly concerned about the needs of all the workers; but those that were hired first thing in the morning felt they were entitled to a better deal. The workers who came to the vineyard early and first, had a sense of being more deserving.

This sense of entitlement is, in my opinion, another major contribution to the current financial crisis.

Some of you may also have had the same experience as I have had, of seeing changes in attitude in some people who become extremely wealthy. It is almost as if a separation occurs from the needs and feelings of the everyday person, delineated by the amount of money one earns. This certainly does not happen across the board. A prime example is the billionaire Warren Buffet who lives in the same house in the central Dundee neighborhood of Omaha that he bought in 1958 for $31,500, today valued at around $700,000.

I believe that chief executives who are paid millions of dollars become insulated from the needs of their average employee. In fact they remind me of the coal barons, the fabulously wealthy owners of the coal mines, at the time of the industrial revolution in my home country Wales.

The coal barons literally owned their employees. They owned the houses in which the miners lived, and the miners were paid with vouchers that could only be used at the grocery stores, that the coal barons also owned.

The coal barons were, like the all day workers in the vineyard; they felt they were entitled to a better life than the everyday person. I do not believe human nature has changed one iota since the time of our Lord, St, Paul or the coal barons in Wales.

Greed; self-interest ahead of the needs of the many; an entitlement to excessive wealth; a fear and lack of trust in God providing for our needs; lack of generosity. I believe all of these human frailties contribute to the current world financial crisis; and they all exist because of a failure to live our lives in a manner worthy of the Gospel of Christ.

At the end of the day we are created by God to love and to give, to be selfless in God's image. We are created to be as generous with others as God is with us.

Staying connected to the community of the body of Christ

The 56th verse of the 6th Chapter of John's Gospel: "Those who eat my flesh and drink my blood abide in me and I in them."

From the very first day we are born, life itself means living in community. When we are connected to each other, in community, we often feel more fulfilled. We feel better in attitude and health; we feel more valuable and more valued; we feel less vulnerable. That is why illness or retirement or harsh disagreement can be so debilitating when those events damage, or break connections with, the communities we love to be part of.

As Christians, from the moment of our baptism, we have lived in a community, but one that differs from other communities in the world because we live not just in communion with each other, but we live our lives in communion with Jesus Christ. Our life as Christians means in community with each other; life by its very nature is plural.

Life is lived together with one another; and Jesus taught us through the sharing of the Bread and Wine that life is shared together and with Him. *"Those who eat my flesh and drink my blood abide in me and I in them"*: Christ dwells in us and we in Him. Jesus, through the sharing of Holy Communion, taught us the value of community, a community that always includes Christ.

I have experienced an illness throughout my life that results, on occasion, in my becoming temporarily disconnected from the communities I love, including my family, my friends, my work and my Church.

From my experience I have a deep and profound understanding of what it feels like to be disconnected from the community I love. I have experienced that even to sit at the dining table with my family, something we did every day of our lives was, when I was in the depths of depression, quite unthinkable. Not to sit with my family, the people who loved me most in the world, was a better alternative to the fear of being with other human beings.

But I have also experienced the joy when the illness fades, and I become reconnected to my loving communities. The joy of learning that however bad the depression was, it could not disconnect me from Jesus Christ.

My battle with depression has taught me many things, but among them is just how important community is. And with my personal experience in mind, for us as Christians to allow single issues to divide us and separate us is quite absurd.

Life is difficult enough for us as a community. Do we really want to draw lines in the sand on issues we don't even fully understand? Lines drawn so that the result is in us being separated from the love of each other and distracting us from the real issues, our relationship with God through our Lord Jesus, and the love of God for all people.

In the sacrament of the Holy Communion, the sharing of the Body and Blood of our Lord, Jesus is binding us, his Community of faith, together with Him. The bonds that link us together are found in Matthew 22, verse 37. Jesus is responding to the Pharisees question as to which is the greatest Commandment.

Jesus said, *"You shall love the Lord your God with all your heart, and with all your soul, and with all your mind. This is the greatest and first commandment. And a second is like it: You shall love your neighbor as yourself."*

Jesus did not teach us to be selective as to which neighbor we love.

This past week has seen a plethora of commentaries and opinions on the homosexuality issues debated at the Minneapolis Episcopal Convention. I have searched objectivity on both sides of the issue and am saddened by the degree of pain experienced by sincere and devoted Christians.

In the midst of the letters and E-mails was a commentary in the Wall Street Journal by Harvey Cox, Professor of Divinity at Harvard. In summing up Mr. Cox says:

> Several other Denominations have been stalling for years on the status of gay Christians in the church. Should they be welcomed at all, or barred at the door? Should they be content with second-class citizenship and excluded from leadership? Should we go back

to pretending they are not there at all when everyone knows they are?

We as Christians need to get past this enervating debate so that we can move on to other pressing issues that require the churches' attention, such as the growing gap between the rich and the poor.

I am not an Episcopalian, but I commend that church for the deliberate way it proceeded to come to a decision about the nagging questions that have paralyzed so many other churches. The rest of us have been set a good example.

A fellow Episcopal deacon reminded me yesterday, "Now that the argument has been decided, and whether or not we agree with the decision, our job is to comfort those who do not understand and who are in pain."

We always need to be there for each other, particularly in times of strong disagreement. We need to remain connected to our community in the way that Christ taught us. Yes, we need different opinions. We need open debate. We as a church can deal with all that.

But above all, we must stay in communion with each other and with Jesus Christ. To love and care for each other no matter what the issue.

Turning your concerns over to God

"'Young man, I say to you, rise!' The dead man sat up and began to speak, and Jesus gave him to his mother."

Today's readings from the book of Kings and the Gospel according to Luke tell similar stories. In both situations God works what appears to us as the unimaginable. Working through the prophet Elijah, Our Father in Heaven raises a human being from the dead to life. Elijah implores, *"O Lord my God, let this child's life come into him again."* The Lord listened to the voice of Elijah; the life of the child came into him again, and he revived.

In the Gospel story today we hear of Jesus also raising a

dead person to life, but with the widow's son Jesus does not implore the Father to help him bring life to the dead. He just says to the dead man, *"Young man, I say to you, rise!"* I believe Jesus knew that he is of God, and that the Father has imparted in him the power to perform such miracles.

In both stories, God is directly invited into the life of the world, to make an incredible difference... to recover the living from the dead.

Some twenty years ago there was a man in his mid-forties, who was the Chief Executive of a 300 physician group at a major teaching hospital in Chicago. This man was very well paid and was thought of very highly by the physicians and the hospital management. The man had considerable experience in healthcare administration and in the space of five years built the physician group into one of the leading managed care providers in the Midwest.

The man's success resulted in other physicians and hospitals' coming to seek his help... and in the man's mind he could solve pretty much any business problem thrown at him. The man was confident that the future would lead to increasing affluence, and that his six figure salary was just the beginning.

As with a number of Jesus' teachings and miracles, in Luke's Gospel we hear today of an action that in many ways parallels the historical actions of the revered Hebrew prophet Elijah. When we are told, *"Fear seized the crowd,"* and they glorified God saying, *"A great prophet has risen among us,"* I believe the crowd's wonder at Jesus' actions. They recalled at once their knowledge of history and compared Jesus with the actions of Elijah.

The crowd clearly recognized this prophet, this Jesus' connection with the Almighty. The crowd had witnessed the power of God coming into the world and causing a great change to occur.

In five years, the 300 physician medical group had grown too fast to be able to support itself. It had taken on too much financial risk, and in the space of twelve months the medical group had fallen from one of the great success stories in the region to facing impending bankruptcy.

The Chief Executive was devastated. He saw his reputation in ruins, and he could not believe that he, with all his experience and education, could not solve the group's problems.

One moment he was his employer's star performer; now he was the dog.

The proud executive laid awake at night, the worries now transitioning from how to solve the group's business problems to how to get out of this totally bad situation without his life collapsing. Eventually, almost inevitably, his health deteriorated. He suffered deep depression; and when he was able to drive downtown his knuckles would turn white from grabbing the steering wheel so tightly, searching his mind trying to solve the dilemma he was in.

In raising the widow's son from the dead, Jesus is showing us that God's power to make a difference in our lives is immeasurable. The power of God's love transforms our lives, just so long as we allow God to enter in and make the change, which for many of us is not that easy to do. To turn ourselves, our lives, our concerns, to turn them over to God frequently contradicts the way we were educated and raised. It is the balance between taking responsibility to effectively manage our lives while at the same time being open to hearing God's word and using the power of His love to make a difference in the world.

The chief executive was asked to resign from his position, in large part because of the incapacity caused by the depression.

But then in the midst of one of the most difficult parts of his life, a miracle occurred that was to change his life forever.

The former chief executive of course was me. In the pit of my professional and personal depression, I was called upon by God to make some serious adjustments to my life.

A close friend, who happens to be an Episcopal priest, advised me, "When you are driving down life's highway at 5 miles per hour in a traffic jam, when you are grabbing the steering wheel so tightly that the blood drains from your knuckles... then you turn your hands over. In so doing, at 5 miles per hour you can still drive using the backs of your hands, but more importantly you are turning your concerns over to God. You are allowing God to help you drive your life. You will have sought His help and His guidance; you will be connected to God in all phases of your life. And," he added, "not just in your visits to Church on a Sunday." My friend went on, "And I have to tell you if this connection occurs, be prepared for some additional major changes in your life."

Both Jesus and Elijah are a connection between God and God's people. Neither of them works what we consider a miracle for his own glory. Their actions glorify God. All who witness these miracles give glory to God and acknowledge that God works through these two men. The widow said to Elijah, *"Now I know that you are a man of God, and that the word of the Lord in your mouth is truth."*

Out of the depths of the worst time of my life came a number of great gifts: my family's unfailing, immovable support, and what was ultimately discerned as God's call to me, to be ordained as a deacon.

At the very time that I was so vulnerable and so depleted, my friend the Episcopal priest asked me if I had ever thought of becoming a deacon. At that time in the fall of 1993, I learned a profound truth; that in the midst of the depths of one's apparent human weakness, if one's heart is open to Him, then the Holy Spirit working through people of faith, God will come into our hearts and our minds and change our lives forever.

One of the lessons we learn from the readings today is

that what Jesus and Elijah did, we must do also. We'll probably not literally raise people from the dead, but we are called to be conduits of God's grace, and we are called to be prophetic. Being prophetic doesn't mean that we have to be dramatic. We are prophetic when we are aware of the needs in the world around us, and we speak the truth about it. The power of prophesy is in the truth of the words, and the challenge those words offer people to change for the better.

That is precisely what happened to me in the fall of 1993. I heeded the prophetic words and advice from my friend, and my life and our family life together changed forever, and it clearly changed for the better.

Thank you, God, for helping us in our time of need. Thank you for reminding us where the true power and wisdom lies, with you, oh God.

Thank you for opening our hearts to you and offering us the opportunity to minister to each others' needs in this world.

Appendix 1

Page   *References to Holy Scripture*

11-14   Job 38:1-11,16-18; Psalm 107:1-32 or 107:1-3, 23-32; 2 Corinthians 5:14-21; Mark 4:35-41; (5:1-20)

15-18   Jeremiah 31:7-14; Psalm 84; Ephesians 1:3-6,15-19a; Matthew 2:1-12

19-25   Exodus 20:1-17; Psalm 19; 1 Corinthians 1:18-25; John 2:13-22

26-31   Isaiah 56:1 (2-5) 6-7; Psalm 67; Romans 11:13-15, 29-32; Matthew 15:21-28

32-37   Jeremiah 14:7-10, 19-22; Psalm 65 ; 2 Timothy 4:6-8, 16-18; Luke 18:9-14

38-42   Daniel 7:9-14; Psalm93; Revelation 1:1-8; John 18:33-37 or Mark 11:1-11

43-47   Exodus 12:1-4, (5-10), 11-14; Psalm 116:1, 10-17; 1 Corinthians 11:23-26; John 13:1-17, 31b-35

48-50   Exodus 12:1-14a; Psalm 78:14-20, 23-25; 1 Corinthians 11:23-26(27-32); John 13:1-15

51-56   Acts 17:22-31 or Isaiah 41:17-20; Psalm 148 or 148:7-14; 1 Peter 3:8-18 or Acts 17:22-31; John 15:1-8

57-60   Exodus 12:1-14a; Psalm 78:14-20, 23-25; 1 Corinthians 11:23-26(27-32); John 13:1-15

61-64   Daniel 12:1-4a (5-13); Psalm 16 or 16:5-11; Hebrews 10:31-39; Mark 13:14-23

65-68   Isaiah 45: 1-7; Psalm 96 or 96:1-9; 1 Thessalonians 1:1-10; Matthew 22:15-22

69-73   Isaiah 59(1-4) 9-19; Psalm 13; Hebrews: 5-12--

6:1, 9-12; Mark 10:46-52

74-77   Jonah 3:10-4:11, Psalm 145, Philippians 1:21-27, Matthew 20:1-16

78-83   Zephaniah 1:7, 12-18; Psalm 90 or 90:1-8, 12; 1 Thessalonians 5:1-10; Matthew 25:14-15, 19-29

84-89   Isaiah 7:10-16; Psalm 80:1-7, 16-18; Romans 1:1-7; Matthew 1:18-25

90-94   Isaiah 40: 21-31; Psalm147: 1-12, 21c; 1 Corinthians 9:16-23; Mark 1: 29-39

95-99   Amos 8: 4-7 (8-12); Psalm 138; 1 Timothy 2:1-8; Luke 16:1-13

100-104 1 Samuel 3:1-10 (11-20); Psalm 139:1-6, 13-18; 1 Corinthians 6:12-20; John 1:43-51

105-108 Isaiah 2:10-17; Psalm 89:1-18 or 89:1-4, 15-18; Romans 6:3-11; Matthew 10-34-42

109-114 Exodus 19:2-8a; Psalm 100; Romans 5: 6-11; Matthew 9:35—10:8 (9-15)

115-118 Acts 1:1-11 or Ezekiel 1:3-5a, 15-22, 26-28; Psalm 47 or Psalm 110:1-5; Ephesians 1:15-23 or Acts 1:1-11; Luke 24:49-53 or Mark 16:9-15, 19-20

119-123 1 Samuel 15:34-16:13, Psalm 20, 2 Corinthians 5: 6-17, Mark 4:26-34

124-128 Deuteronomy 15:7-11; Psalm 112; 2 Corinthians 8:1-9, 13-15; Mark 5:22-24, 35b-43

129-134 Jeremiah 23:1-6; Luke 1:68-79 or Psalm 46; Colossians 1:11-20; Luke 23:33-43

135-139 Joel 2:23-32 or Sirach 35:12-17 or Jeremiah 14:7-10, 19-22; Psalm 65 or 84:1-7; 2 Timothy 4:6-8, 16-

18; Luke 18:9-14

140-145   1 Samuel 16:1-13; Psalm 23; Ephesians 5: (1-7) 8-14; John 9:1-13 (14-27) 28-38

146-149   1 Samuel 3: 1 - 10; Psalm 63: 1 - 8; 1 Corinthians 6: 11b - 20; John 1: 43 - 51

150-153   Isaiah 43:18-25; Psalm 32 or 32:1-8; 2 Corinthians 1:18-22; Mark 2:1-12

154-158   Acts 13:44-52 or Leviticus 19:1-2, 9-18; Psalm 145 or 145:1-9; Revelation 19:1, 4-9 or Acts 13:44-52; John 13:31-35

159-162   Zechariah 9:9-12; Psalm 145 or 145:8-14; Romans 7:21-8:6; Matthew 11:25-30

163-167   Acts 16:9-15; Psalm 67; Revelation 21:10, 22–22:5; John 14:23-29

168-171   Proverbs 9:1-6; Psalm 147 or 34:9-14; Ephesians 5:15-20; John 6:53-59

172-176   Acts 8:26-40 or Deuteronomy 4:32-40; Psalm 66:1-11 or 66:1-8; 1 John 3:(14-17) 18-24 or Acts 11:19-40; John 14:15-21

177-180   Exodus 16:2-4, 9-15; Psalm 78:1-25 or 78:14-30, 23-25; Ephesians 4:17-25; John 6:24-35

181-186   Acts 2:42-47; Psalm 23; 1 Peter 2:19-25; John 10:1-10

187-192   1 Kings 19:4-8; Psalm 130; Ephesians 4:25-5:2; John 6:35, 41-51

193-198   Isaiah 62:1-5; Psalm 36:5-10; 1 Corinthians 12:1-11; John 2:1-11

199-203   Isaiah 43:18-25; Psalm 41; 2 Corinthians 1:18-22;

Mark 2:1-12

204-207   Job 38: 1-11, 16-18, Psalm 107: 1-32, 2 Corinthians: 5 14-21, Mark 4: 35-41

208-212   Joel 2:1-2, 12-17 or Isaiah 58:1-12; Psalm 51:1-17; 2 Corinthians 5:20b-6:10; Matthew 6:1-6, 16-21

213-217   Genesis 18:20-32; Psalm 138; Colossians 2:6-15; Luke 11:1-13

218-220   Jeremiah 17:5-10; Psalm 1; 1 Corinthians 15:12-20; Luke 6:17-26

221-224   Genesis 15:1-6; Psalm 33 or 33:12-15, 18-22; Hebrews 11:1-3 (4-7) 8-16; Luke 12:32-40

225-228   Exodus 12:1-14a; Psalm 78: 14-20, 23-25; 1 Corinthians 11:23-26 (27-32); John 13:1-15

229-233   2 Samuel 11:1-15 and Psalm 14; or 2 Kings 4:42-44 and Psalm 145: 10-19; Ephesians 3:14-21; John 6:1-21

234-237   Isaiah 40:1-11; Psalm 85:1-2,8-13;2 Peter 3:8-15a; Mark 1:1-8

238-242   Exodus 34:29-35; Psalm 99; 2 Corinthians 3:12-4:2; Luke 9:28-36, (37-43)

243-246   Deuteronomy 8:7-18; Psalm 65; 2 Corinthians 9:6-15; Luke 17:11-19

247-251   Exodus 16:2-15, Psalm 105:1-6, 37-45; Philippians 1:21-30; Matthew 20:1-16

252-255   Proverbs 9:1-6; Psalm 147 or 34:9-14; Ephesians 5:15-20; John 6:53-59

256-261   1 Kings 17:8-16 (17-24) or 1 Kings 17:17-24; Psalm 146 or 30; Galatians 2:15-21; Luke 7:11-17

Appendix 2
About the author and illustrator

Reverend John Dolan

The Reverend John Richard Dolan was born in Oxford, England, and was raised close to the ancient Cathedral in Llandaff, Wales. John has lived and worked in the United States for 40 years

John is a British Chartered Accountant (CPA) and is an ordained Deacon in the Episcopal Church USA. This unlikely combination and his having lived in two very distinct cultures has given John the opportunity to discern his spiritual journey from differing perspectives.

"The Mushroom Farm" is John's first book and the stories are based in large part on sermons given over nearly fifteen years service as a Deacon...

John has been married to his wife Karen for more than 34 years. They have a married daughter Michelle and son David. The Dolans have three grandchildren.

Paul Joshua Egel

The Illustrator of the "Mushroom Farm," Paul Egel, is a Chicago native and a professional artist/illustrator. Paul received his BFA from Long Beach State University, California. Other places of study include Griffith Univeristy in Brisbane, Australia, and College of DuPage, Glen Ellyn, IL. More of his work can be viewed at: www.egelart.com

www.ingramcontent.com/pod-product-compliance
Lightning Source LLC
Chambersburg PA
CBHW032104090426
42743CB00007B/227